IMAGES
of America

NAPA VALLEY
WINE COUNTRY

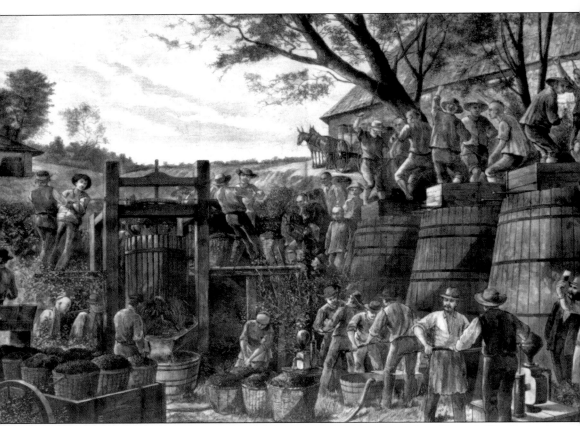

P. Frenzeny's fanciful rendering of a California wine crush appeared in *Harper's Weekly* in the 1880s. The wine press here is like those used in small wineries, but wine makers would have laughed at the notion of barefoot Chinese stomping on the grapes. Easterners knew that the Napa Valley was a major viticultural center, and they knew that Chinese laborers came to California to help build the railroad. They were not aware of the anti-Asian prejudice common in rural areas like the Napa Valley.

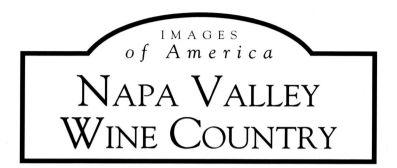

IMAGES
of America
NAPA VALLEY WINE COUNTRY

The Napa Valley Museum and Lin Weber

ARCADIA
PUBLISHING

Published by Arcadia Publishing
Charleston, South Carolina

Printed in the United States of America

Library of Congress Catalog Card Number: 2004100107

For all general information contact Arcadia Publishing at:
Telephone 843-853-2070
Fax 843-853-0044
E-Mail sales@arcadiapublishing.com
For customer service and orders:
Toll-Free 1-888-313-2665

Visit us on the Internet at www.arcadiapublishing.com

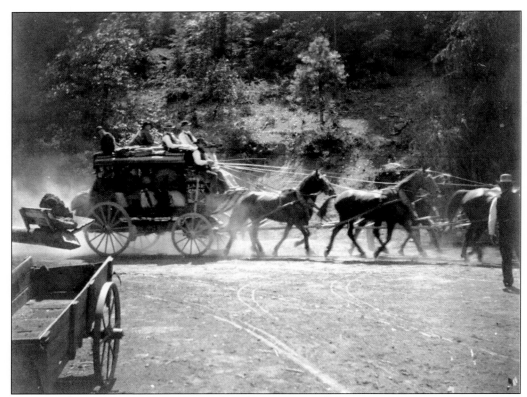

"The roads are dusty and almost beyond endurance."—William H. Brewer, 1861.

CONTENTS

ACKNOWLEDGMENTS

Thanks . . .

The Napa Valley Museum is proud to present *Napa Valley Wine Country*. The production of this book could not have been possible without author Lin Weber's hard work, dedication, knowledge, and commitment to the cultural heritage of the Napa Valley. A former Museum trustee, she is one of the Valley's most accomplished historians and authors. There is no one more qualified to put together this collection of the Museum's historic photographs.

Our thanks, too, go out to the Sharpsteen Museum, the St. Helena Historical Society, the St. Helena Public Library, the Napa County Historical Society, the Napa Valley Vintner's Association, and the Wine Library Association for allowing us to have access to their photographic collections.

The Museum is grateful to the hundreds of people who have donated pictures, scrapbooks, and illustrations to our archives over the years. Through their generosity we have become a repository for the cultural and historical legacy of the region. Preservation of this legacy continues to be one of the most significant aspects of our mission. It is our hope that through projects like this one, residents and visitors to the Valley will develop a better sense of place, which will inevitably lead to a stronger appreciation for the region.

I would also like to acknowledge Arcadia Publishing and editor Hannah Clayborn for their willingness to publish *Napa Valley Wine Country*. We are pleased to join the many hundreds of other museums and historical societies throughout the United States that have worked with Arcadia in producing their highly acclaimed *Images of America* series.

Sincerely,

Eric Nelson, Executive Director
The Napa Valley Museum

INTRODUCTION

In a world where the big, the fast, and the new reign supreme, the things that are small, slow, and old-fashioned may seem of little value. There have been times when some in the Napa Valley yearned for a slick modernity, but most of these efforts have proven futile or, worse, have backfired disastrously—especially in the Up Valley, the region known today as the Wine Country.

Entrepreneur Sam Brannan may have been the first to experience this fact of life. Brannan made a mint during the Gold Rush by selling supplies to the miners at exorbitant prices. He tried to repeat the feat in Calistoga, the resort spa he established at the head of the Valley. He filled it with wonders, like a long fence made of petrified wood, a silkworm farm, a Druid temple, and a brewery employee who was said to have eaten several members of the Donner Party. These enticements failed to lure. Few people came to his resort.

Refusing to give up, Brannan and some local politicians conspired to build a railroad to the resort, at taxpayers' expense. The project was completed with hype and fanfare, but the line failed to thrive and died along with the spa. Leland Stanford finally bought both the railroad and the resort. Along the way, however, and pretty much by accident, Brannan founded the sweet, lovely little city of Calistoga.

The inspiration for building his elaborate vacation getaway probably came from the town called "Hot Springs," a tiny community of merchants and farmers some 12 miles to the south. Hot Springs was a collection of modest stores that grew up near another spa, White Sulphur Springs, where wealthy San Franciscans retreated from the pressures of their busy lives to "take the waters" and eat well beneath soaring redwoods in fashionable seclusion. The town eventually changed its name to "St. Helena," after the mountain that dominated its landscape to the north.

A few pioneers succeeded in planting fruit and nut trees and sold their harvest to the gold miners who were swarming into the Sierras, but the soil around St. Helena and Calistoga was considered poor: thin, often clayey, and cursed with an overabundance of volcanic rocks. Most people who hoped to make fortunes as farmers eventually moved away.

About the same time that Brannan was building his resort, a handful of St. Helenans experimented with a venture that hitherto had attracted little interest in America—winemaking. Two men led the way in this. One was Charles Krug, a charismatic former German newspaper editor whose political views were considered radical in the Old Country. He had gone into partnership in a gold refining enterprise with Agostin Haraszthy, vintner for the Mexican general who administered the Napa Valley when it was part of Mexico. When the smelting business failed, Haraszthy showed Krug how to make wine. Krug invested everything he had and more into the wine business. He owned vast amounts of land and planted grapes wherever he could. He was a friend to all, but died bankrupt. Most consider him to be the father of the Napa Valley wine industry.

The other leader was George Beldon Crane, an Alabaman. Crane was a trained physician, but he retired from medicine to become a banker. He lent money, charged interest to pioneer ranchers all over the Bay Area, and rode long miles on horseback to collect on the debts. Crane was well educated and had a scientific mind. He determined that the soil around his home was ideally suited for grape growing and shared his findings in letters and articles in several publications. Crane kept careful watch over his plantings, his wine, and his finances, and he eventually abandoned viticulture when it failed to be profitable. He died wealthy, but unloved by many, and his contributions to the industry have been largely ignored.

Inspired by the expansive Krug and edified by the intellectual Crane, farmers planted grapes all over the Up Valley. Some with actual winemaking experience, like Jacob Beringer, came to the Valley to ply their trade. The clever got rich, not as much through the grapes they grew and brewed, as through real estate transactions. The price of land soared. Scores of merchants opened shops in St. Helena, each touting larger selections, lower prices, and better quality than the other (but never all three at the same time). Wealthy visitors and locals who emulated their lifestyle helped the merchants prosper. Business owners built elegant stone buildings, and the rural town took on an air of European refinement.

St. Helena's bubble burst when the economy in general faltered and a tiny but devastating little bug slowly invaded the vineyards. Deeply concerned that the Napa Valley was losing people and revenue, the county decided to install a big, fast, new convenience: an electric train running the length of the Valley. The electric line, they hoped, would stimulate growth. It didn't.

When public opinion turned against the alcoholic beverage industry and Congress voted in Prohibition, the little city of St. Helena couldn't even pay its electric bills. Hailed at first as "the greatest piece of moral legislation in history," the Volstead Act was repealed in 1932. But it was too late. St. Helena, Calistoga, and the other towns in Napa Valley's wine country slipped into a kind of slumber. When they awoke, they found that modern times had passed them by.

This was, they eventually realized, a very good thing. Small, slow, and old-fashioned turned out to be very appealing attributes, and the citizens of the Wine Country have gone to great lengths to keep it that way ever since.

In 1968 Napa County voted in a landmark law protecting agricultural land from developers. The wine industry took off like a shot. Big corporations and small investors snatched up Napa Valley real estate and entered the wine business. In the 1980s, a number of world-class restaurateurs also came to Napa Valley, raising the quality of life to dizzying new heights. A new group of Hispanic laborers also came. Now they participate fully in the life of the Up Valley's communities and play a vital role in the life of the Wine Country.

One

THE FIRST

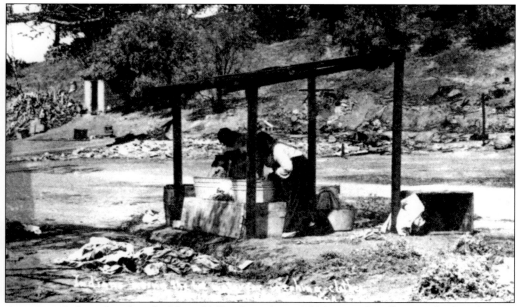

American Indians lived in the Napa Valley for at least 6,500 years. Smallpox and other diseases nearly obliterated them, and many of the survivors withdrew to their ancestral home further north. Here, Indian women wash clothes at a hot spring in Calistoga. Before Europeans discovered the Napa Valley in 1823, native people only wore clothes in the winter, and those were made of fur or grass. (Courtesy of the Sharpsteen Museum.)

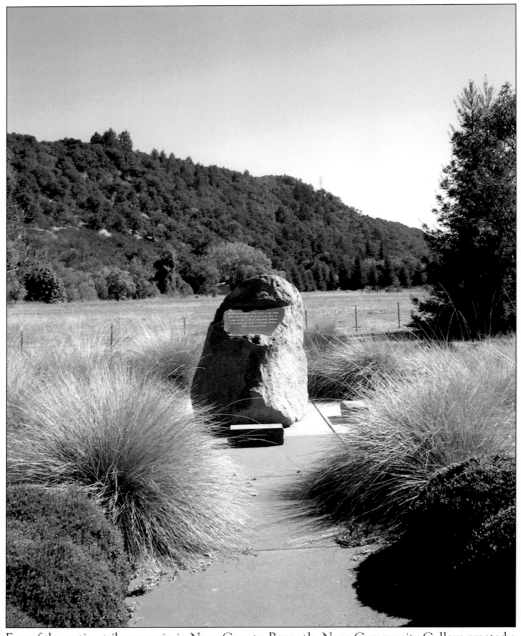

Few of the native tribes remain in Napa County. Recently, Napa Community College erected a monument in their memory at its St. Helena campus. The engraving says:

Oh great spirit whose voice I hear in the wind,
Whose breath gives life to the world, hear me.
I come to you as one of your many children.
I am small and weak, I need your wisdom.
May I walk in beauty.

Generalissimo Mariano Vallejo was the chief administrator of the territory when the Napa Valley belonged to Mexico. Believing that settlers would keep the region safe from Indian raids and occupation by foreign powers, he bestowed grants of land to people he favored. Mariano was humane, with a great love of family and people in general. After California became a state, he was elected to the state senate, and the city of Vallejo bears his name.

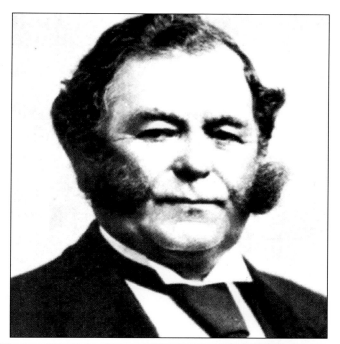

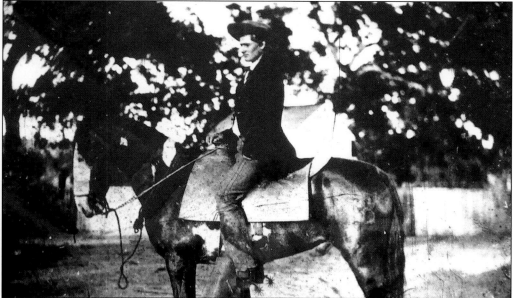

Edward Turner Bale, seen here in this ambrotype astride his horse, was born in England about 1810. He served as physician to Mariano Vallejo and the Mexican army, but his favorite medicine was alcohol. He was once arrested for dispensing it from his office. Bale married a niece of Mariano's brother in 1841. Her dowry consisted of an enormous grant of land, 17,000 acres that stretched from the northern boundary of Rutherford to what is now Tubbs Lane in Calistoga. He called it "Rancho Carne Humana," a pun on the Indian word *Callejomano*, which was the name of a semi-permanent encampment on his rancho. Bale died in 1849, not long after this picture was taken.

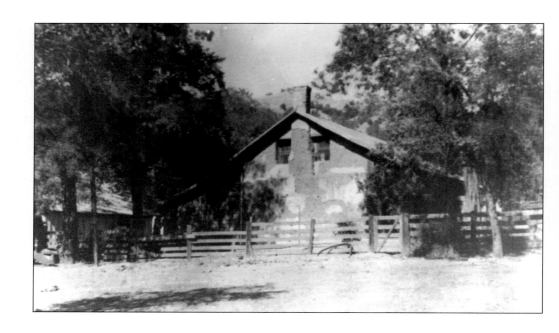

In 1841 the first group of potential American settlers, known to historians as the Bartelson-Bidwell Party, breached the High Sierras, which Californios (people living in California when it belonged to Mexico) thought were impassable. Vallejo gave a land grant to one in the party, Joseph Ballinger Chiles, (*right*) in 1843, on the condition that Chiles build a mill for him. Chiles called his grant "Rancho Catacula" and built the large adobe house seen above. He later moved to Rutherford and then to St. Helena.

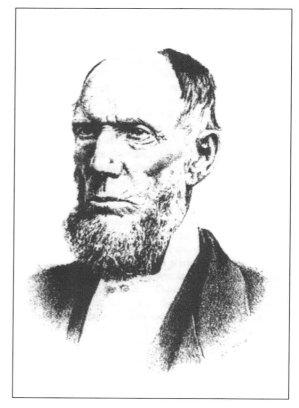

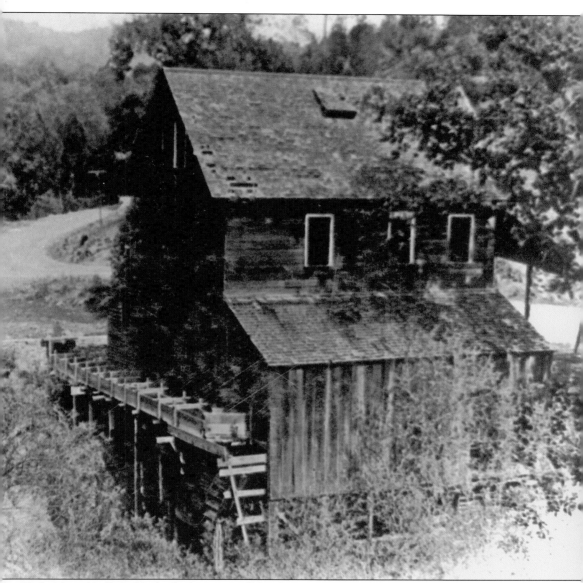

Chiles' friend Billy Baldridge built a gristmill, but his original intention was to construct a sawmill for processing the timber that grew around Catacula and in the neighboring ranchos, Locoallomi and Carne Humana. He tried to haul a huge band saw to California but had to abandon it in the desert when it became stuck in the sand. It rusted away, busted apart, and for a time looked, from a distance, vaguely like a pachyderm's trunk. Its appearance gave rise to the query whispered by awestruck gold miners: "Have you seen the elephant?" As Mariano Vallejo had hoped, the gristmill on Rancho Catacula attracted other pioneers, who settled and grew wheat and other grains. Chiles, Pope, and Berryessa Valleys served as regional breadbaskets throughout the Civil War. Chiles also built a whiskey distillery, which made him the first producer of retail alcohol in Napa County. He marketed both the wheat and the booze under the "Catacula" label.

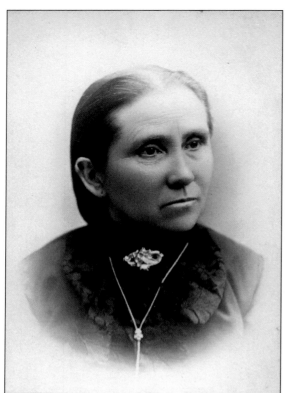

A widower, Joseph Chiles left his children in the care of friends when he came to California to find a new life. He made two trips back to Missouri to reunite with his children and escort them west. He married again, this time to Margaret Jane Garnhart, seen here.

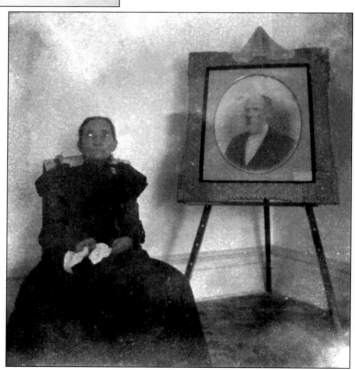

Margaret revered her husband, Joseph Chiles, long after he passed away.

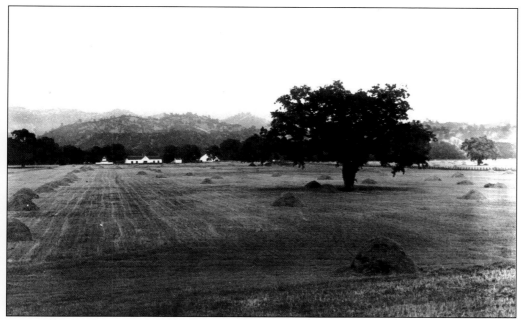

General Vallejo granted two brothers in the high-ranking Berryessa family, Jose Jesus and Sisto, eight square leagues of rich agricultural land in the eastern part of what later became Napa County. They called their grant Las Putas (the whores), probably a pun on the Indian name for the creek that ran through the area, Putah. In the picture above, a grain harvest is piled into hive-shaped stacks.

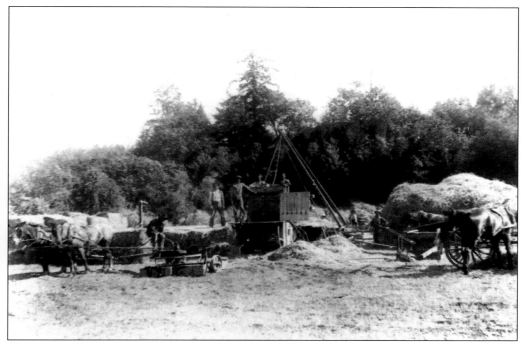

Threshers in Berryessa shake the grain from the chaff.

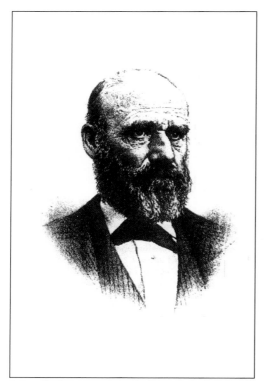 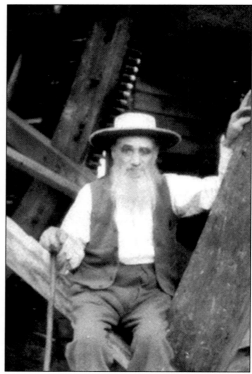

John York arrived with his extended family in 1844 as part of a new wave of American settlers. He went to work splitting fence rails for Dr. Edward Bale. The upper Napa Valley had one of the highest concentrations of U.S. citizens in all of Northern California in the early 1840s. York, called "Dean" by his friends and family, lived to be 90. He and his wife, Lucinda Hudson York, populated the area with numerous other Yorks, and members of the family are still making contributions to the communities of the Napa valley.

The picture on the right shows him seated in the old Bale Mill, long after the mill's wheel stopped grinding.

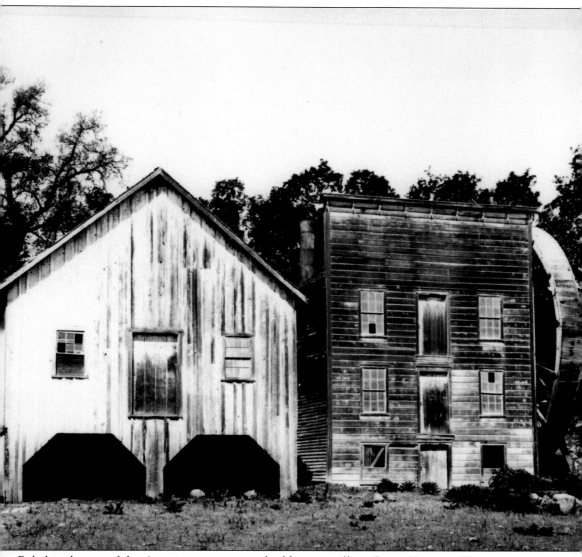

Bale hired some of the American pioneers to build a gristmill on Carne Humana. To power it, they built flumes and diverted streams from Spring Mountain. The mill's presence helped the new settlers form a community. Gristmills were crucial to the social development of rural areas in the mid 19th century. Besides providing the practical necessity of grinding grain into flour, mills were a meeting place for farmers, whose homes were often miles apart. Building the mill brought together many of the Up Valley men, and gave their wives and children a chance to socialize. The pioneers also built a granary for the mill, a small church, and a schoolhouse, the second American school in all of California (established July 1847). They also constructed a sawmill, but most of the wood used in each of these projects was planed by hand. (Photo by Henry Lewelling; Courtesy of the St. Helena Public Library.)

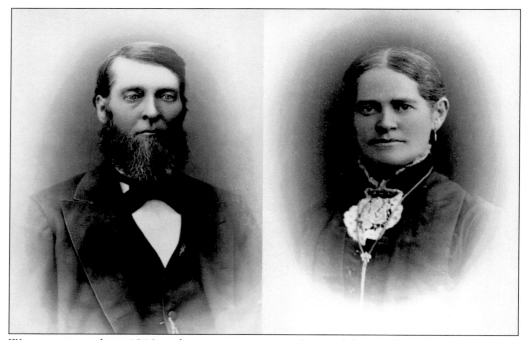

Winter came early in 1846, and it was a stormy one. Some of the overland pioneers that year lingered before crossing the mountains. John Cyrus and his family just missed being snowed in, but the Graves family, part of the Donner Party, was trapped in the Sierras. Lovina Graves lost several members of her family to starvation. John and Lovina eventually married and settled near what later became Calistoga. (Courtesy of the Sharpsteen Museum.)

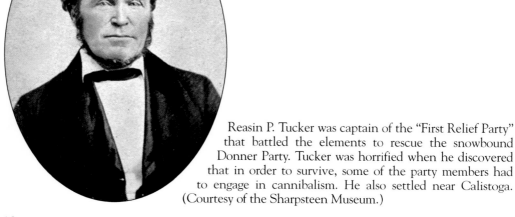

Reasin P. Tucker was captain of the "First Relief Party" that battled the elements to rescue the snowbound Donner Party. Tucker was horrified when he discovered that in order to survive, some of the party members had to engage in cannibalism. He also settled near Calistoga. (Courtesy of the Sharpsteen Museum.)

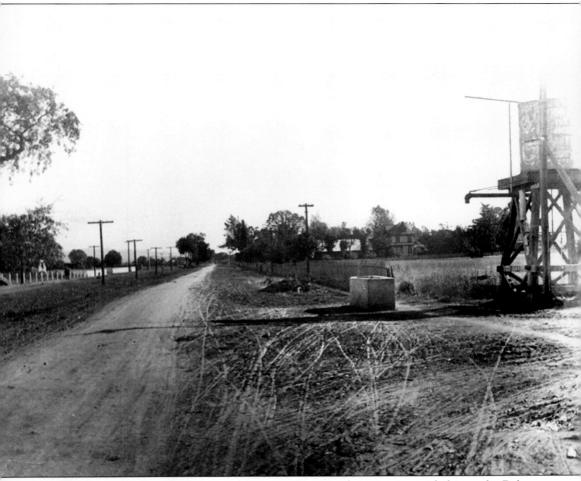

Pioneer Florentine Kellogg had ironworking experience and came west with his tools. Bale asked him to take charge of the mill-building project. In payment, he accepted a large tract of land. Kellogg became a leader in the developing community. At his own expense, he built a series of water towers along the County Road, for the relief of horses and their owners. One of them is shown here. Unfortunately, when challenged in court, Kellogg could not prove that he held legal title to the land Bale gave him. He was forced to move away in the 1870s.

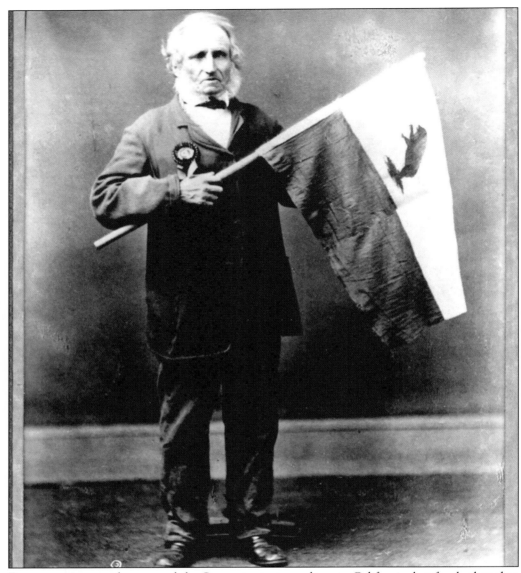

Every year more settlers crossed the Sierras to start new lives in California, but few bothered to get travel passports from the Californio administrators. Angered by this apparent invasion, the Mexican authorities demanded that the newcomers leave. In 1846 matters came to a head, and many of the pioneers in Napa and Sonoma Counties decided to take matters into their own hands. They gathered recruits and met at the Bale Mill on Saturday, June 13, 1846, to plan their attack. The next day, the settlers seized the Californios' headquarters in Sonoma. A Danish sailor named Peter Storm (above) claimed to have drawn the flag that the rebellious settlers flew over Vallejo's garrison. The figure on the flag is a bear, and the rebels called themselves the "Bear Flaggers." The Mexican-American War, which was already underway in the Southwest, spread into California and finally ended in 1849 with the United States as victor. The Bear Flag is now the state flag of California (although the bear is walking, not rearing for attack). Storm carried the flag in Napa County parades for decades after California became a state. It is now buried with him in his coffin at the Tulocay Cemetery in Napa. (Courtesy of the Sharpsteen Museum.)

Two

THE HOT SPRINGS

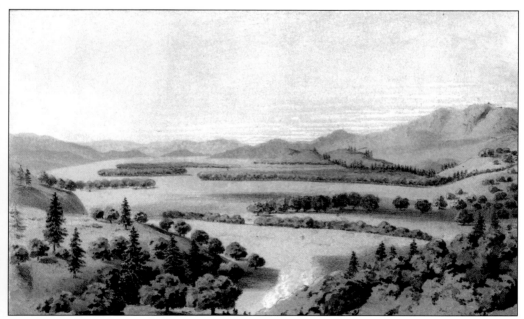

The painter of this *c.* 1852 Napa Valley landscape shows the Upper Valley's hot springs in the foreground. The artist omitted the Napa River.

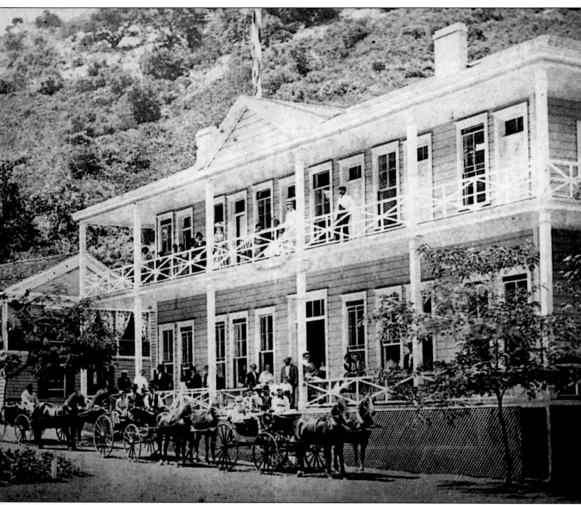

With money they had made during the Gold Rush, David Hudson and John York purchased land near what later became St. Helena. While exploring their new possession, they came upon some hot springs in a secluded setting, redolent with the smell of sulphur, a mineral that was thought to be healthful. They sold the land to a developer, Leonard Lillie, and in 1852 "White Sulphur Springs," California's first resort spa, opened for business.

On May 16, 1854, business partners J. Henry Still and J.J. Walters bought 126 acres from Edward Bale's widow, Maria, planning to start a town near the White Sulphur Springs resort. Its location would be at the junction of the road to Pope Valley (in the hills to the northeast) and the road that bisected the Napa Valley from Napa to the Bale Mill and beyond. John Scott Kister (at right) was the first to set up shop. He opened a shoe and boot-making enterprise and a fix-it shop on the corner of what would later become Main and Spring Streets. They thought the name of the new village would be "Hot Springs Township."

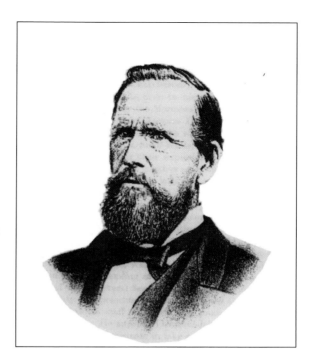

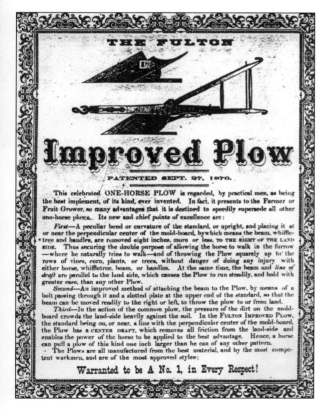

David Fulton was a saddle maker with a business on Main Street, but he tried other pursuits as well. He invented a special offset one-horse plow that won awards at the State Fair.

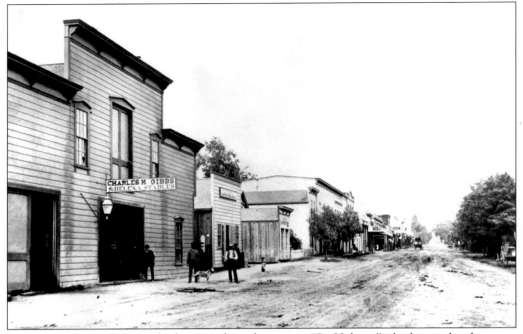

By the early 1860s the town had acquired another name, "St. Helena," which was also the name of the local chapter of the Sons of Temperance, a fraternal organization promoting abstinence from alcohol. Charles Gibbs's stables bore the town's name. (Courtesy of John York.)

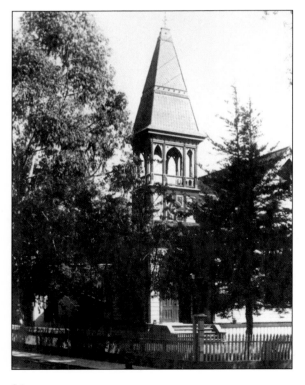

Many of the earliest pioneers were Southerners. They started Sharon Baptist church on what became known as Church Street in St. Helena.

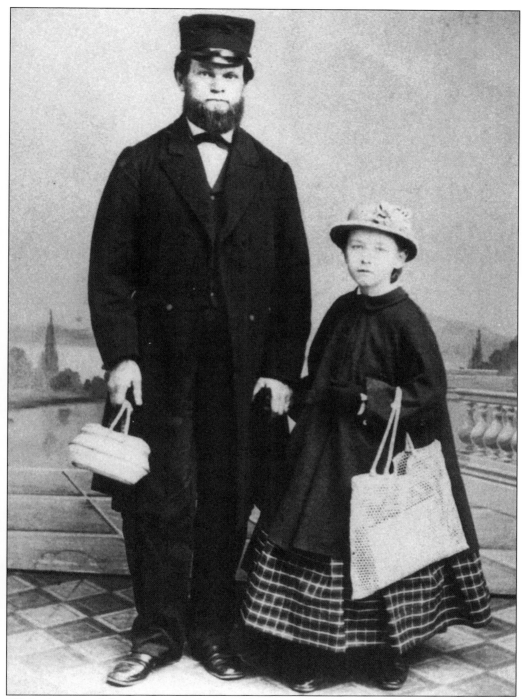

While the rest of the country was fractured by a great Civil War, Californians relaxed in hot springs resorts. Sven Alstrom, an experienced hotelier, bought White Sulphur Springs. Its popularity soared. Sven is shown here with his daughter Sophie who became an accomplished artist and married the local Presbyterian minister, John Mitchell.

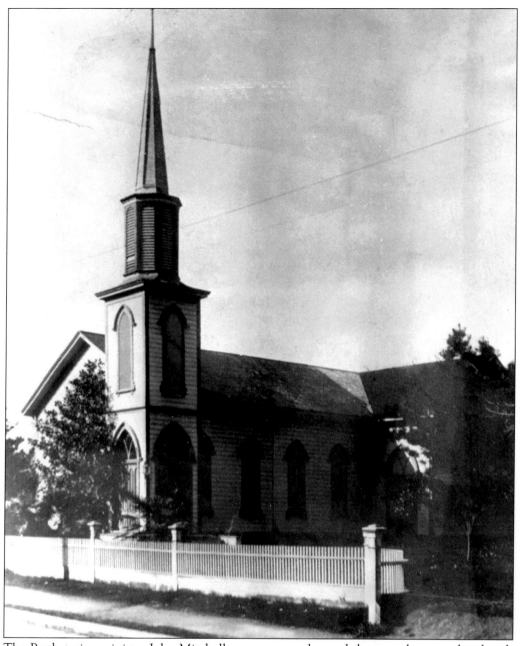

The Presbyterian minister John Mitchell was very popular, and the attendance at the church soared. His reputation was enhanced by his charming wife, Sophie Alstrom Mitchell, of White Sulphur Springs.

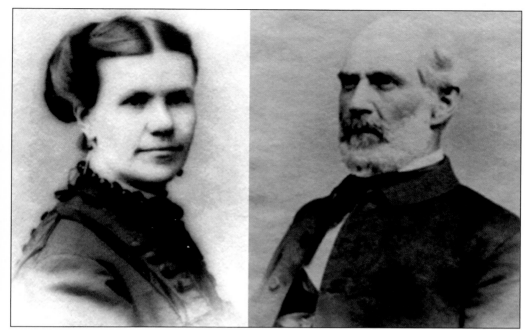

William Bourn and his wife, Sarah, were so fond of White Sulphur Springs that they bought land nearby and built a second home there. Bourn was a partner in the Empire Gold Mine. He accidentally shot and killed himself while preparing for a payroll trip to the mine. After Will's death, Sarah spent much time in St. Helena and was very involved in the Episcopal Church, to which she gave generously.

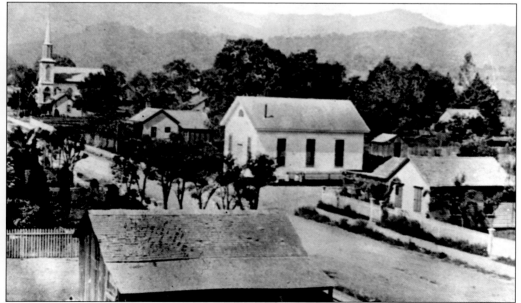

Other denominations also built churches. This picture of Spring Street in the late 1860s shows the Presbyterian Church on the left and, in the center, the Catholic Church, which was cold, drafty, and too small for its congregation. The Catholics sold it to the Episcopalians in the 1870s.

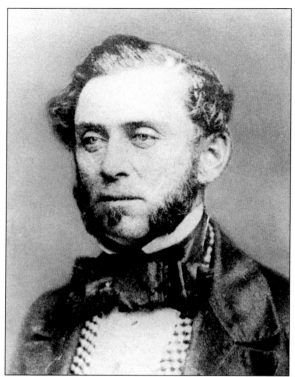

Sam Brannan, editor/publisher of a San Francisco newspaper, made a fortune in the Gold Rush—not as a miner, but as a supplier of goods for which miners had to pay very high prices. He sent an issue of his newspaper to China urging Chinese laborers to come to California. Then he cornered the market on tea. Chinese men came by the thousands, drank the tea, and stayed to build the railroads.

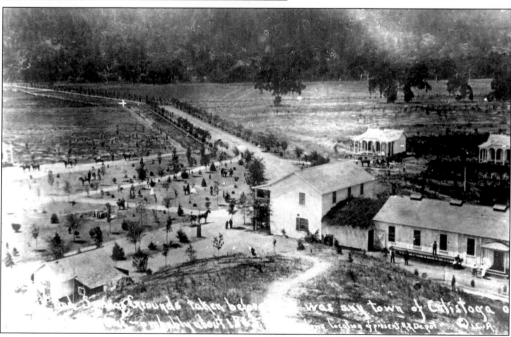

Brannan wanted a resort of his own. Brannan's Hot Springs, established in 1865, was at the head of the Valley, where springs of hot water bubbled up from the ground. The city of Calistoga now occupies the acreage shown here.

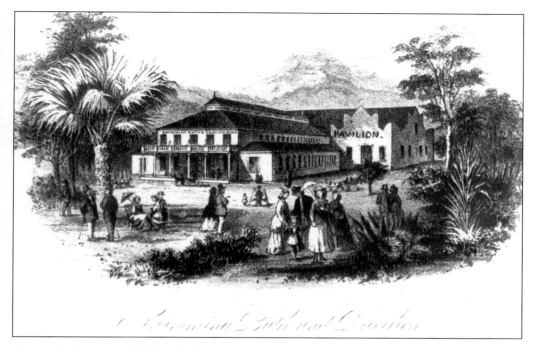

Brannan's Swimming Bath and Skating Rink may have been especially appealing to women, because they are in the majority in both scenes. The fence traversing the apparently swampy land in the picture below was made—all or in part—of petrified wood gathered from the hills to the west of Calistoga.

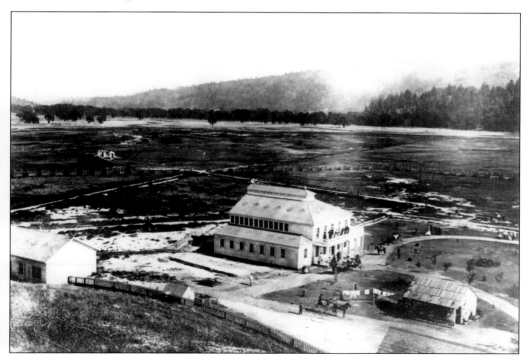

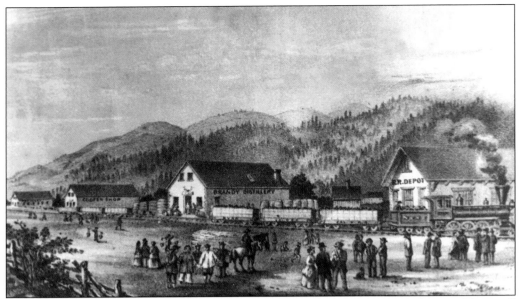

Three Chinese men stand in the foreground (left of center) of this artist's rendering of the small industries at Brannan's Calistoga Hot Springs Resort. Chinese laborers are hauling baskets with poles over their shoulders elsewhere in the picture. The Chinese settlement in Calistoga was south of the railroad station.

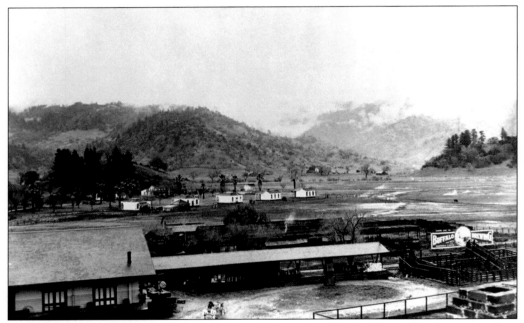

Brannan had a brewery, a distillery, and eventually a winery. He hired Louis Keseberg to work at the distillery. Keseberg had been a member of the ill-fated Donner Party and, in one of the young state's first felony trials, was tried for cannibalism and for stealing Tamsen Donner's money. He was acquitted. This photo, taken from the rooftop of a hotel, shows the distillery. Guest cottages are in the background, and the steam rising from the ground is from the hot springs.

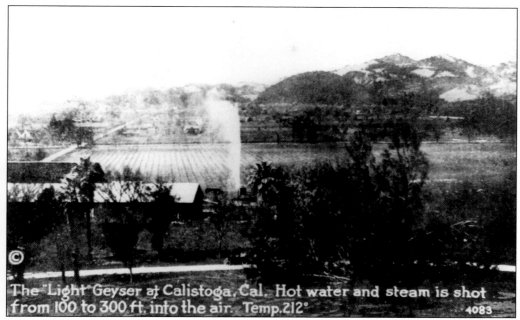

The "Light" Geyser at Calistoga, Cal. Hot water and steam is shot from 100 to 300 ft. into the air. Temp. 212° 4083

Brannan hoped that curiosities like this geyser and a fence made of petrified wood from a forest of ancient fallen trees a few miles away would lure visitors. Later, Ephraim Light and his family owned the geyser.

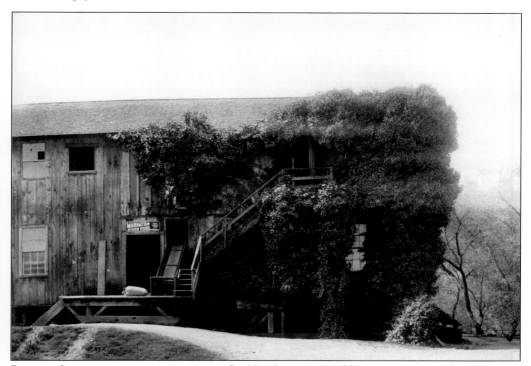

Brannan began numerous enterprises at the Hot Springs. In addition to commonplace ventures like this mill, he also tried growing tea and raising silkworms.

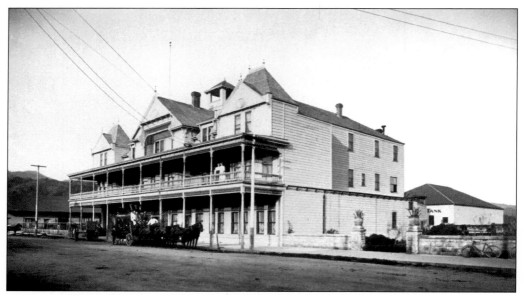

Visitors to Brannan's resort had to endure a long stagecoach ride from the wharf in Napa, more than 40 miles to the south. The roads were rutted and dusty in the summer and a miry mess in the winter. Patrons at the Calistoga Hotel could enjoy mud and mineral baths, which may have been a welcome relief after the ride up there.

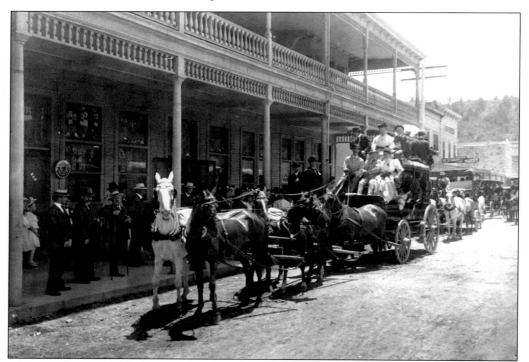

"There is much travel," wrote William Brewer in his journal, "and every team moved in such a cloud that it was impossible to see . . . at any distance—you only saw a cloud of dust." These travelers hope to be first in line, thereby avoiding some of the load of dust.

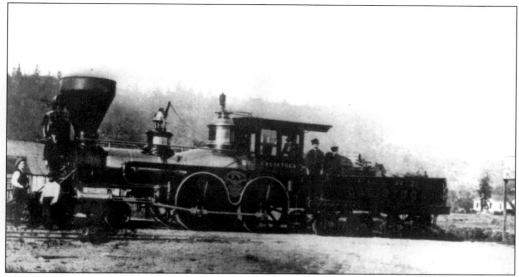

Brannan's solution to the transportation problem was to conspire with a local politician, Chancellor Hartson, to build a railroad to the doorstep of the resort at taxpayers' expense. In their own way, Hartson and Brannan were among the first of the railroad barons. Even though Napa Valley voters nixed the railroad plan, Brannan and Hartson pushed it through anyway. The line bisected many farms, and the railroad put up fences to keep animals away, grossly inconveniencing the farmers. Seen here is the line's first locomotive, the "Calistoga," a wood-burning steam engine. The railroad eventually went broke and was purchased by the Southern Pacific.

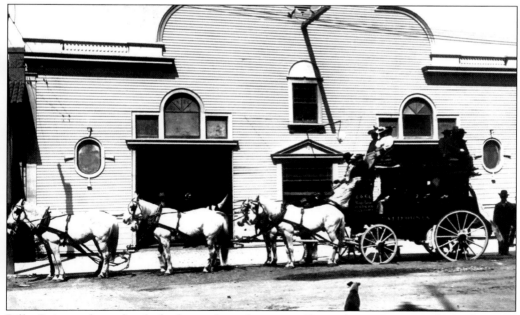

Billy Spiers, whose family had raised racehorses in Kentucky, came west about the time of the Civil War. Spiers dominated the Calistoga—Lake County route for decades. This stagecoach has taken on passengers at Spiers's stage depot. The "C & CL" insignia on the side stands for "Calistoga and Clear Lake."

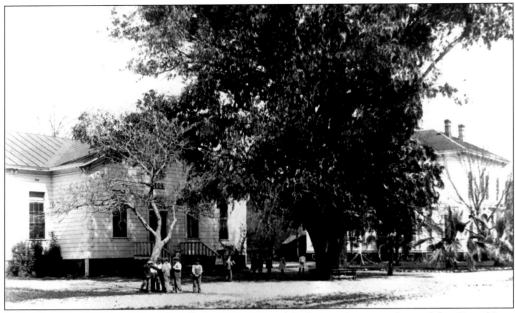

Built in 1869, this Calistoga schoolhouse was in terrible shape when members of the Grand Jury reviewed local educational facilities in the early 1900s, when this picture was taken. Children attended anyway, but few advanced beyond the sixth grade.

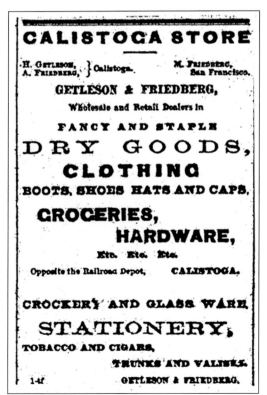

CALISTOGA STORE

H. Getleson,
A. Friedberg, } Calistoga.   M. Friedberg,
                                  San Francisco.

GETLESON & FRIEDBERG,

Wholesale and Retail Dealers in

FANCY AND STAPLE

DRY GOODS,

CLOTHING

BOOTS, SHOES HATS AND CAPS,

GROCERIES,

HARDWARE,

Etc. Etc. Etc.

Opposite the Railroad Depot,   CALISTOGA.

CROCKERY AND GLASS WARE,

STATIONERY,

TOBACCO AND CIGARS,

TRUNKS AND VALISES.

1-tf   GETLESON & FRIEDBERG,

The Calistoga Hot Springs Resort did not make the money Brannan hoped it would. There was a silver strike on Mt. St. Helena that might have prompted a revival of the enterprise. A little town popped up near the silver mine, but it went bust when the mine did. The tiny town's original name may have been Getleson, named for Henry Getleson, Calistoga's first shopkeeper, who had a branch store there. Shopkeeper Henry Getleson and his partner, Morris Friedberg, ran this ad in the Calistoga newspaper for their general store, the first in Calistoga.

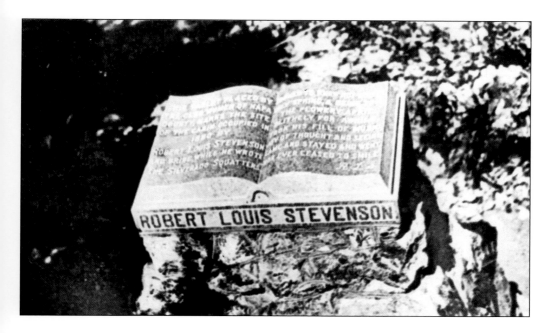

Author Robert Louis Stevenson honeymooned in the ghost town at the mine and wrote about it in his classic book, *The Silverado Squatters*. He gave the town the fictional name, "Silverado." A monument to Stevenson (*above*) is on the flanks of Mt. St. Helena. Stevenson also wrote about the tollhouse at the head of the mountain pass over Mt. St. Helena (*below*). John Lawley, who built the road and enjoyed a prosperous career, lived there in his old age with his daughter, Molly Lawley Patten.

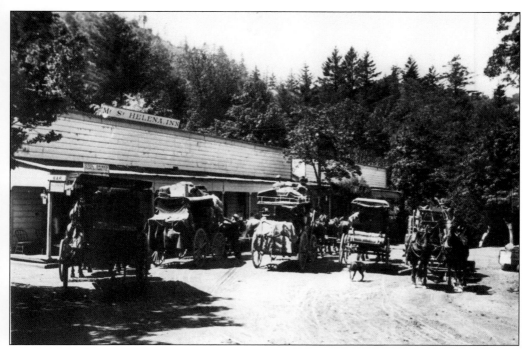

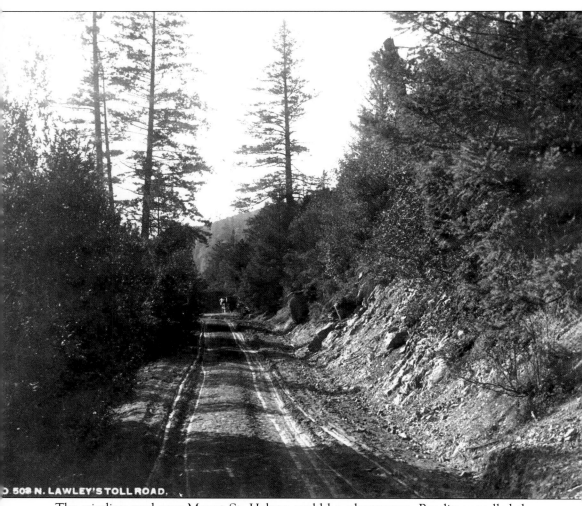

The winding road over Mount St. Helena could be adventurous. Bandits patrolled the area. After robbing the stage just above the Toll House in 1890, for example, James Berkeley, Joseph Morgan, and a third man "holed up" on the mountain until a posse flushed them out. The suspects fled (probably on horseback) to Tubbs Road and then over the hills to Knights Valley before Berkeley and Morgan were captured. The third man got away.

Three

MINING

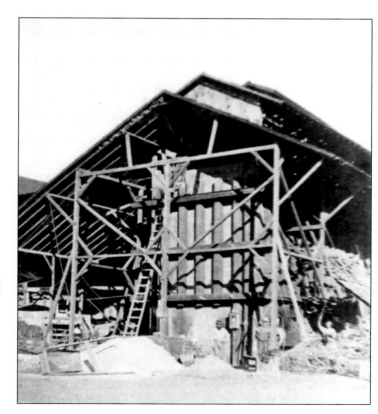

Quicksilver mining was profitable during the Gold Rush because refiners used the highly toxic metal to separate gold from its matrix. This mine was in Knoxville, in the far northeastern part of Napa County. Two workers are in the lower right-hand corner of the picture.

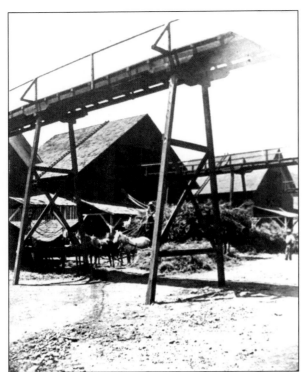

Knoxville was very hot in the summertime, and the heat of the furnaces made the environment almost unbearable. Here, horses bring brush to fuel the fires.

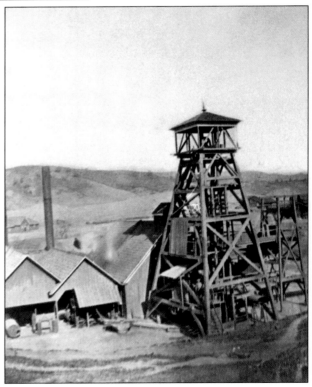

The hoisting works at the RQ Mine lifted ore to be tumbled down for processing.

Chinese laborers worked at these furnaces at the RQ mining company in Knoxville. The work was dangerous and unpleasant. Toxic fumes from the quicksilver could rot teeth and cause brain damage, and job-site deaths were common.

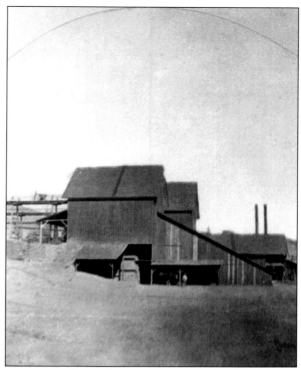

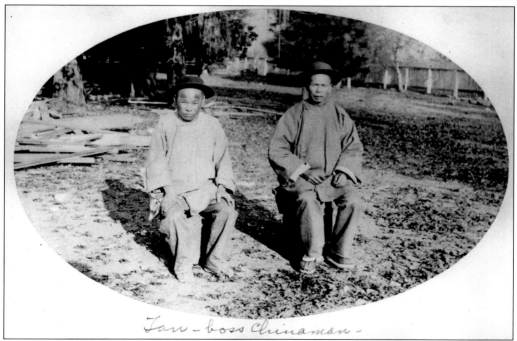

Chinese laborers did most of the heavy work in the mines and other industries. They hauled rock and built many of the stone walls that still exist throughout the Valley. Seen here are two labor bosses.

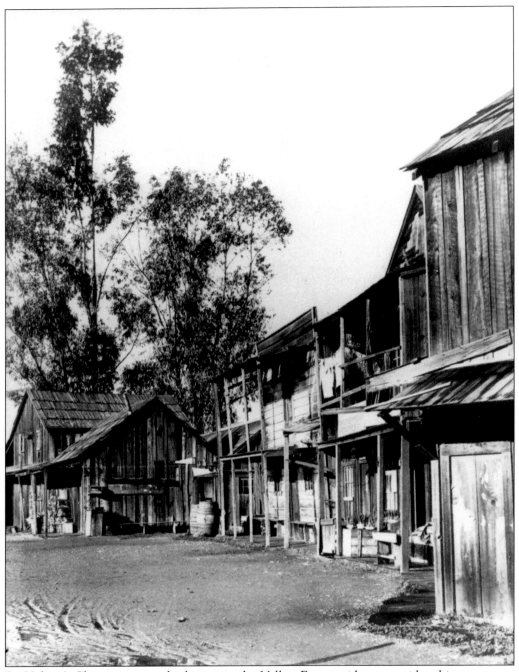

St. Helena's Chinatown was the largest in the Valley. Fussy residents considered it an eyesore and urged its landlords to tear it down. Their objections were founded in anti-Asian prejudice. The Chinese were crucial to the local economy in the late 19th century because they did so much of the heavy labor.

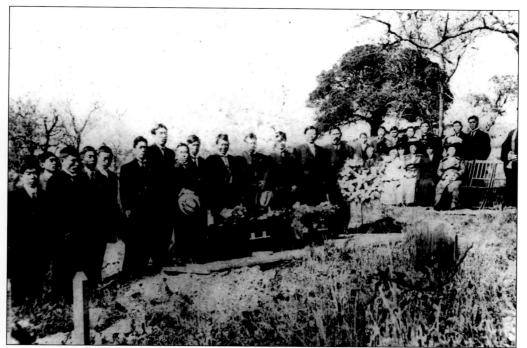

Some Chinese laborers have gathered for a funeral. Most Chinese wanted their mortal remains to be shipped back home to China when they died.

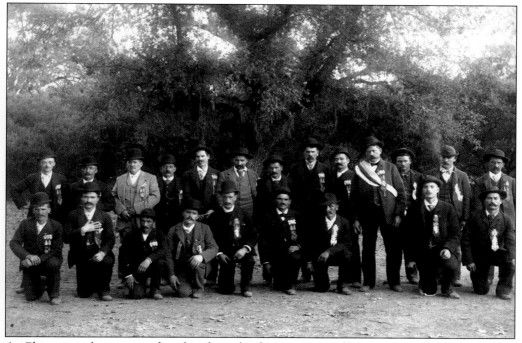

As Chinese workers returned to their homeland a new group of laborers moved into the Valley, the Italians. The Sons of Italy was a popular men's fraternal organization.

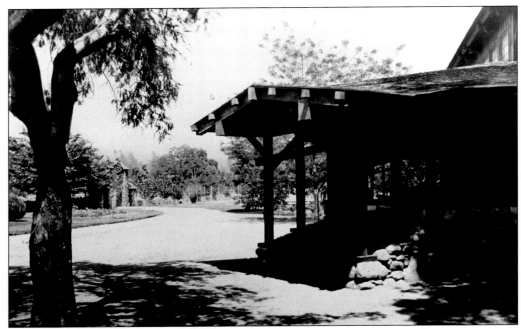

Railroad mogul and politician Chancellor Hartson tried to develop a quicksilver mine in Pope Valley in the 1870s, but he had to close it down because warm underground springs overheated the mineshafts. He turned the place into a resort. The nine-hole golf course he put there was one of the very first in California and is still in operation.

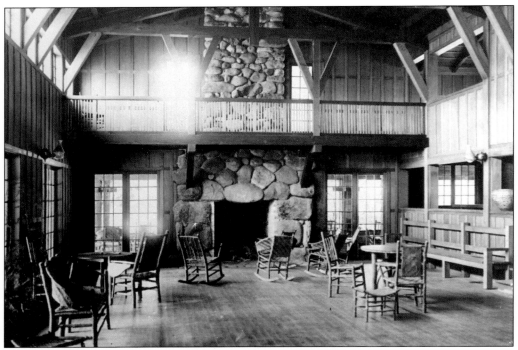

Architect Bernard Maybeck designed the buildings at Aetna Springs.

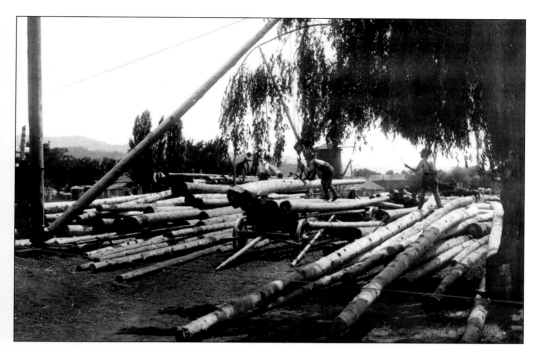

Local lumber companies logged the hills around Calistoga and shipped the wood to Napa. Horses brought the lumber to flatbed cars at the railroad depot in Calistoga. Life as a workhorse was hard and often short, as it was for many of the humans who labored alongside them.

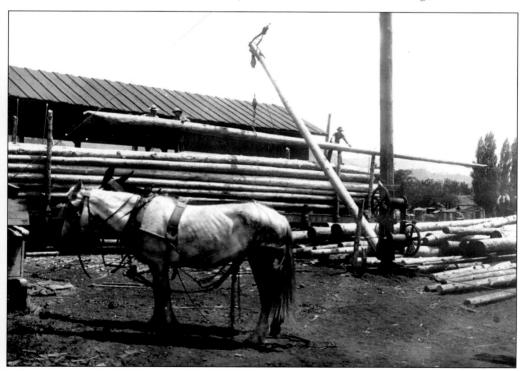

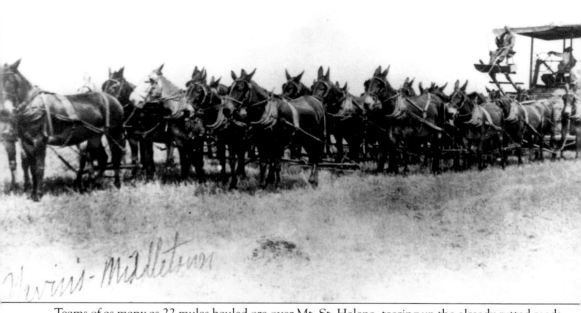

Teams of as many as 22 mules hauled ore over Mt. St. Helena, tearing up the already rutted roads. Shipments were often delayed in the rainy winter months due to the poor condition of the roads.

Four

THE WINERIES

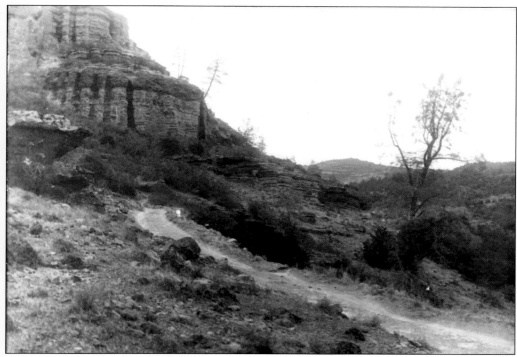

The Palisades (upper left) are the remains of explosive volcanoes that erupted violently some 3 to 5 million years ago. Volcanism was responsible for shaping the landscape of the Napa Valley, creating the mercury and silver deposits, and making the soil perfect for growing wine grapes.

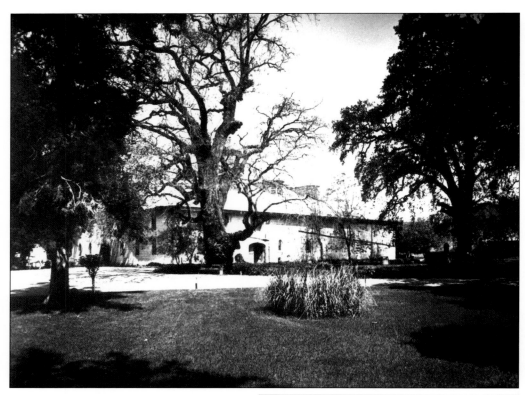

Charles Krug, a political radical who fled
Prussia in 1852, tried publishing and gold
refining before he became a vintner. He
helped a Napa Englishman, John Patchett,
crush 2,000 gallons of wine in 1858.
The next year he made 5,000 gallons for
pioneer George Yount. In 1860 he married
Edward Turner Bale's daughter Carolina,
whose dowry consisted of 540 acres of
prime vineyard land. Krug's winery (*above*)
still bears his name.

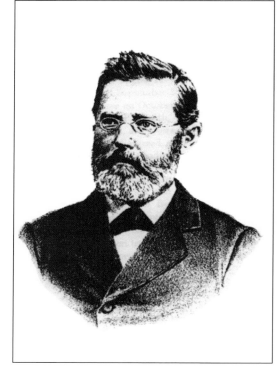

George Beldon Crane, a physician, entrepreneur, and agnostic, lent money to farmers and small businessmen throughout the Bay Area. He parlayed some of the interest he made on these accounts into a purchase of land not far from White Sulphur Springs. He was among the first to plant grapes and may have been the first in the Up Valley to build a wine cellar. This photo was taken in 1863 and may have been on his passport. He traveled to New York during the Civil War, accompanying a shipment of his wine. (Courtesy of Susanne Salvestrin.)

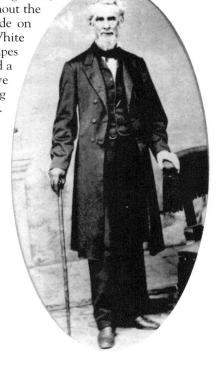

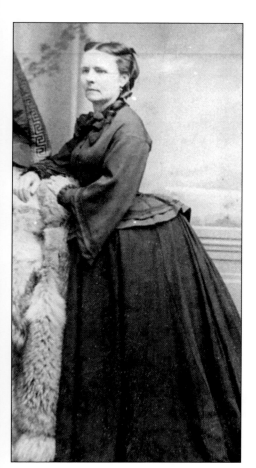

Frances Grayson Crane endured long, lonely days while her husband, George, was away on business, but she enjoyed much prestige among her contemporaries. She is shown here in a dress with a bustle, fashionable in the 1890s.

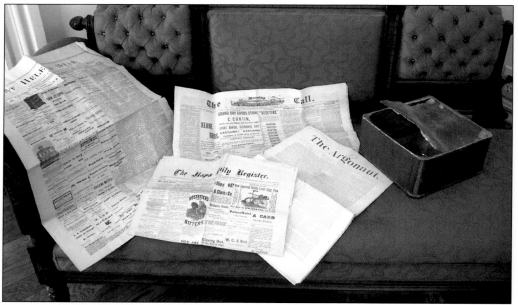

Crane recorded his business transactions in a small diary. This entry, written on Saturday, February 4, 1859, reports that his employee Henry Pellet pruned Joe Chiles's vineyards and got 10,000 cuttings. Pellet had begun to "heal them in," or cover them with soil, the day before. "I do but little eating or sleeping in this region." he writes. (Courtesy of Susanne Salvestrin.)

Crane contributed articles about viticulture to several newspapers. When the Cranes built the addition to their home, they put the newspapers shown here in the square "time capsule," which was tinned at a local hardware store.

This unusual photograph reveals the interior of the Cranes' home. The map of the United States above the table reflects George's taste and interests, but probably not Frances's, although the hatbox on the table may have been hers. (Courtesy of Susanne Salvestrin.)

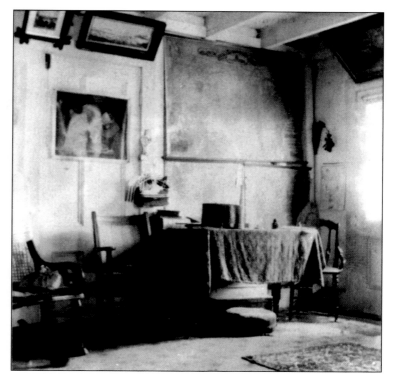

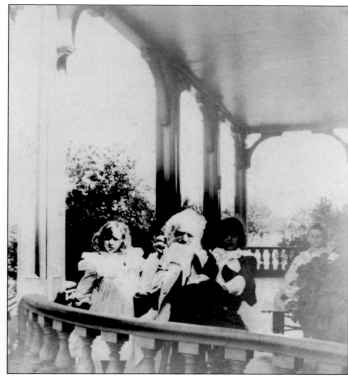

Crane and his great grandchildren celebrate his 91st birthday on the front porch at "Sunny Acres" in 1897. Alice Mary Lemme (left) and Grayson McPike (right) are in the foreground, and Hazel McPike is seated behind them. The Lemmes and McPikes were also pioneer vintners. (Courtesy of Susanne Salvestrin.)

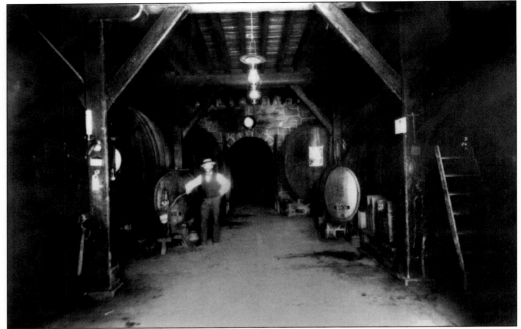

The Beringer family had been in the winemaking business in Germany for several generations. Jacob Beringer (shown here doing a barrel tasting) came to St. Helena in 1868 and worked for a time as Charles Krug's cellar master. His brother Frederick joined him in 1883. They employed Chinese laborers to dig a tunnel in the volcanic tuff behind their winery.

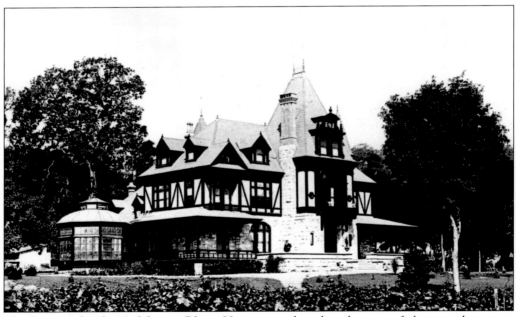

The Beringer brothers' elaborate Rhine House contributed to the aura of elegance that many associated with the wine industry. Frederick Beringer enjoyed his botanical garden in the solarium to the left of the building.

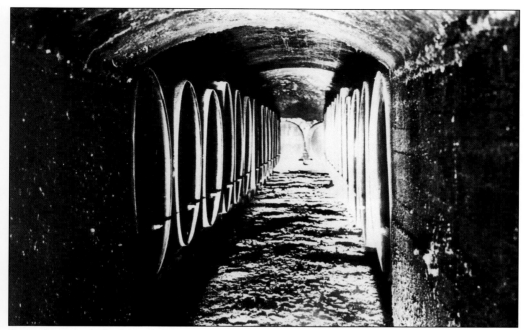

Tunnels in the hillside at the Grimm Winery kept the wine at a cool, even temperature.

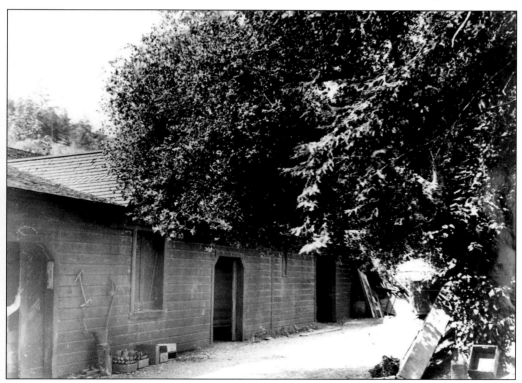

Like many vintners, J. Grimm built his Calistoga winery against a hill. It is now the site of the Storybook Winery.

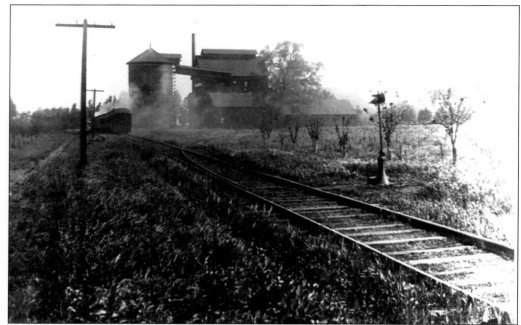

Brun and Chaix's Nouveau Medoc, known to many as the French American Winery, made a red wine that was very popular in the New Orleans market. In this picture a Southern Pacific train steams past. Trains could use the side spur to take on loads.

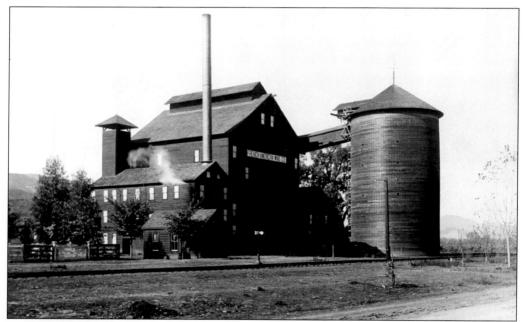

Brun & Chaix built a watchtower (left side of building) so that they could communicate with men working at their vineyard, which was many miles away up Howell Mountain. The winery eventually became part of the California Wine Association (CWA), the huge wine trust of pre-Prohibition days.

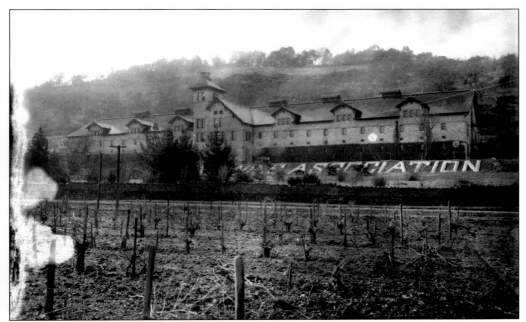

William Bourn's son and heir, Will Jr., built Greystone, the largest building of its kind at that time, to process and store wine from small, private vintners. Greystone became an affiliate of the California Wine Association. Time has damaged this photograph, but it is possible to read the words, "California Wine Association," on the slope in front of the winery.

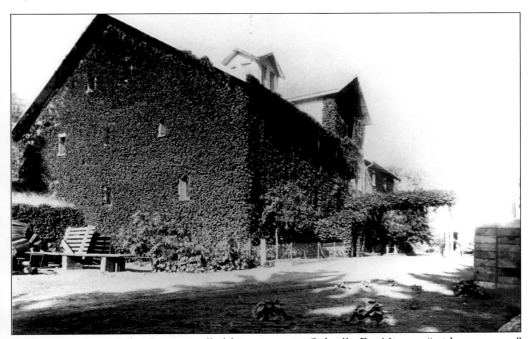

Real estate tycoon John Benson called his winery in Oakville Far Niente, "without a care." Architect Hamden McIntyre designed it, and several other wineries in the Valley.

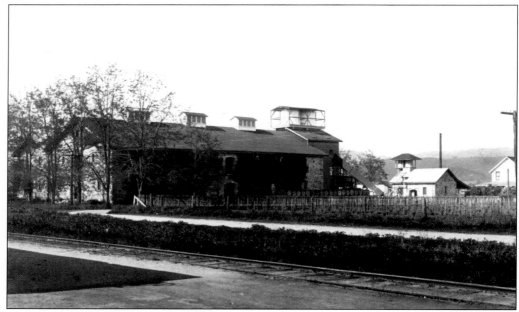

The F.S. Ewer Winery in Rutherford, also designed by architect McIntyre, was a major wine producer in the 1880s. The stone building helped keep the aging wine at a steady temperature. Ewer went into partnership with J.B. Atkinson, who lived nearby.

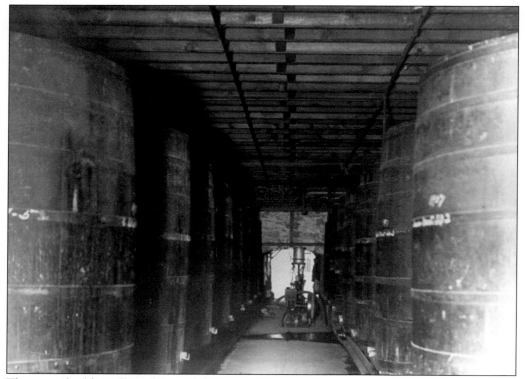

This stone building allowed Ewer-Atkinson's wine to age at an even temperature.

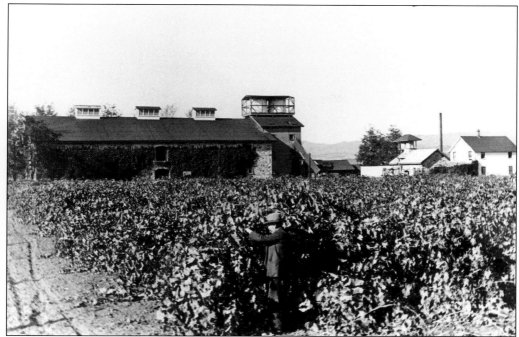

State Senator Seneca Ewer was a founding member of the St. Helena Viticultural Club, where pioneer winemakers and vineyardists shared information and promoted each other's endeavors. Winegrowers rarely planted their vines in neat rows like today's growers do. Different varietals were planted together and crushed together to make blends. There were no trellises.

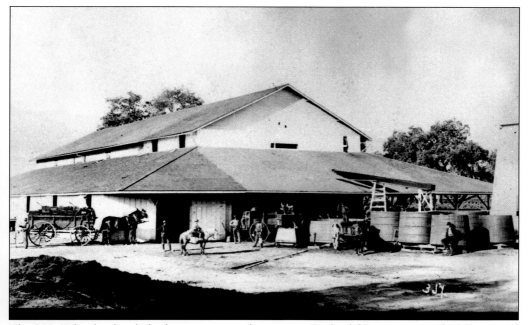

The J.H. Wheeler family had a winery on what is now Zinfandel Lane, near today's Raymond Winery. A young Bill Wheeler rides the pony.

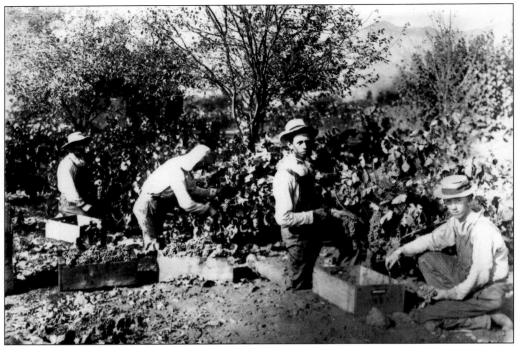

Grape pickers on Spring Mountain harvest the crop.

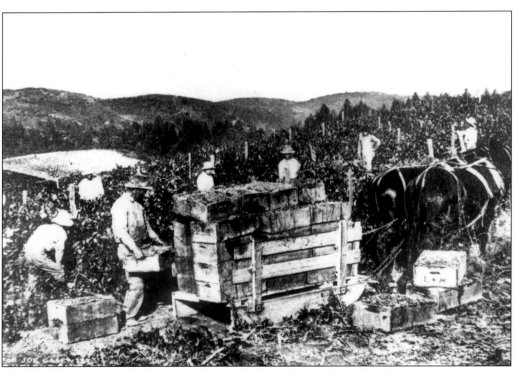

The filled lugs were stacked on a wooden sled, which horses dragged to the cart.

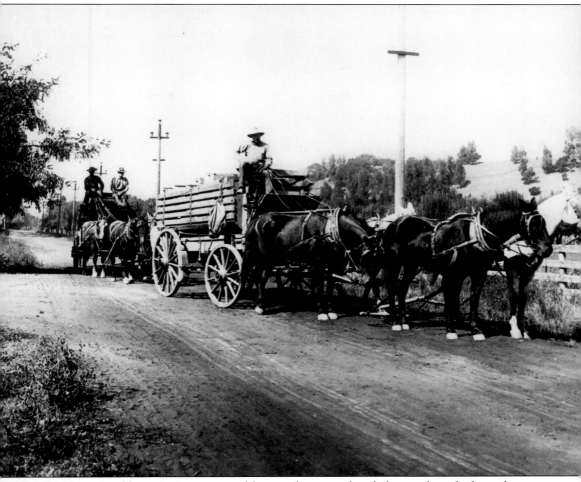

The climate was colder a century ago, and harvest began and ended several weeks later than today. These grapes were on the way to the crusher.

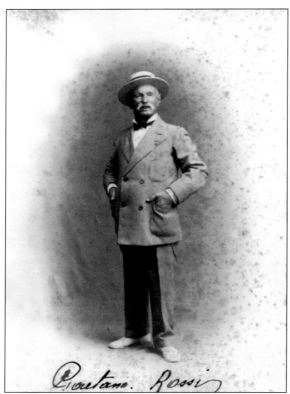

Gaetano Rossi (*left*), seen here in later life, and Louis Vasconi Sr. operated a saloon, the Europa. Rossi left St. Helena for a time. The large structure on the lower left was Rossi's Europa House. A load of wine is being delivered to the William Tell Saloon across the street. Italians frequented the Europa while the Swiss liked the William Tell.

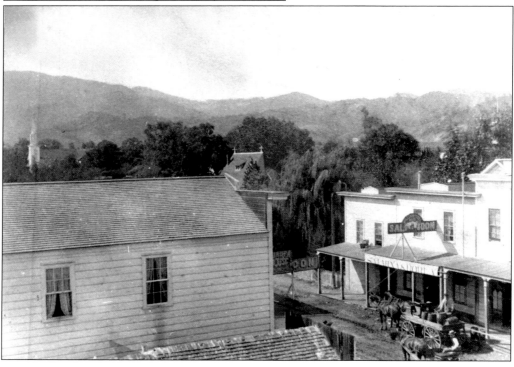

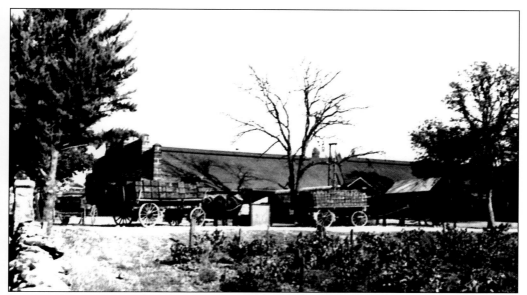

In 1898 Antonio Forni bought a small, redwood wine cellar, the Tychson Winery, south of Calistoga. Gaetano Rossi returned to St. Helena about that time and supervised the construction of a stone building around the original cellar. Rocks quarried from nearby Glass Mountain formed the walls. Forni's Lombarda Winery, named for his birthplace in Italy, produced Chianti and other Italian-style wines. Lombarda later became Freemark Abbey.

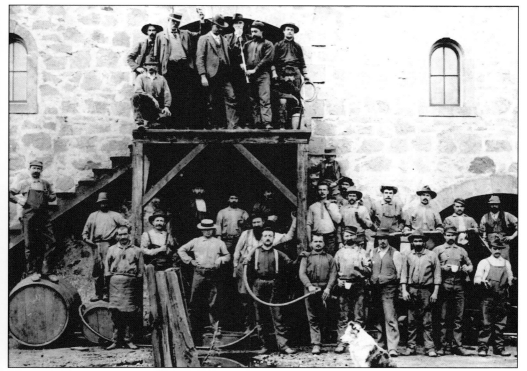

The Forni winery, now Freemark Abbey, employed an enthusiastic staff.

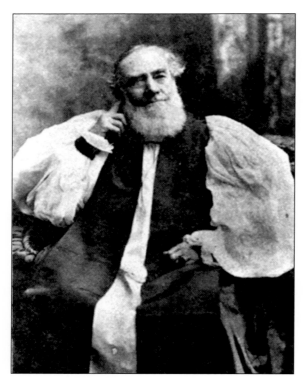

Many were attracted to the Napa Valley because of the aristocratic lifestyle associated with wine making. Rev. Theodore B. Lyman, rector of Trinity Episcopal Church in San Francisco, bought land north of St. Helena, but left it to his son Will when he accepted the call to become bishop of North Carolina. Will planted grapes and started a small winery, El Molino, which means "the mill." The Lymans' vast acreage included the Old Bale Mill, in operation from 1846 until the early 1900s. It stood as a silent relic of days past until being refurbished in modern times.

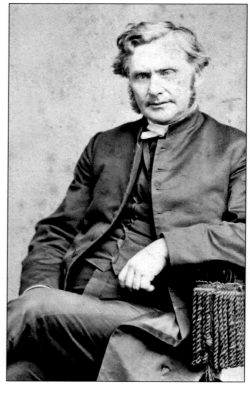

Reverend H.W. Beers, another rector of Trinity Church who bought land down the road, from Reverend Rev. Lyman planted grapes. He stored his wine at Greystone and at the Tychson Winery across the street. His home was located on what is now vineyard land belonging to Ehlers Lane Winery

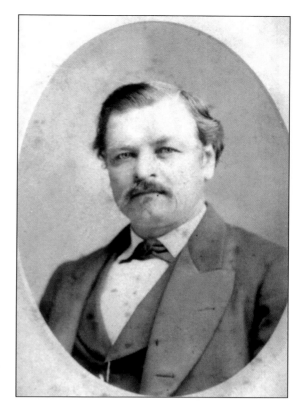

Fritz Rosenbaum (*right*) was a very successful manufacturer and importer of mirrors and fine glass. He worked in San Francisco and found the Napa Valley Wine Country to be a fine place to spend his free time and extra money. His home is now the St. Clement Winery. A camera poised on the Rosenbaums' veranda in the 1880s faces north (*below*). Other vineyards can be seen as darker patches in the distance.

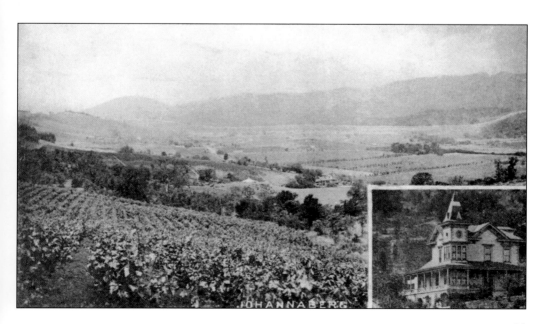

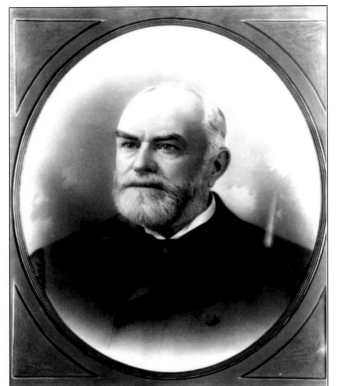

Alfred C. Tubbs, owner of the Tubbs Cordage Company, made a fortune manufacturing string. Many who knew him described him as a "sweet, gentle man," despite his grim look in this picture. He built a magnificent home just north of Calistoga, on what is now Tubbs Lane (*opposite page, top*). The rocks used to build his turreted, castle-like winery (*below*) were probably quarried nearby, as were the rocks used to build the bridge leading up to his grand estate (*opposite page, bottom*). In the 20th century his winery became Chateau Montelena.

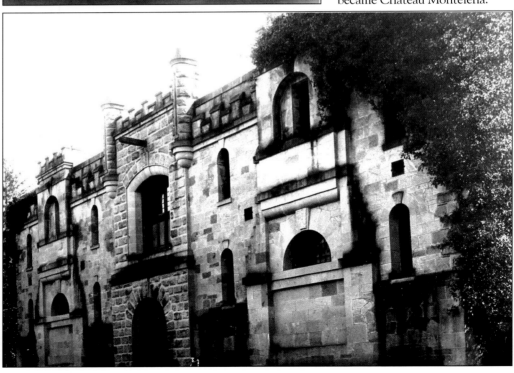

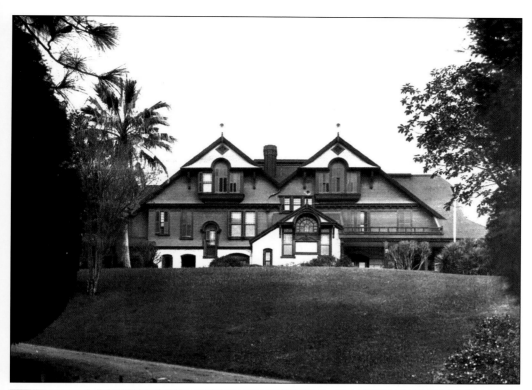

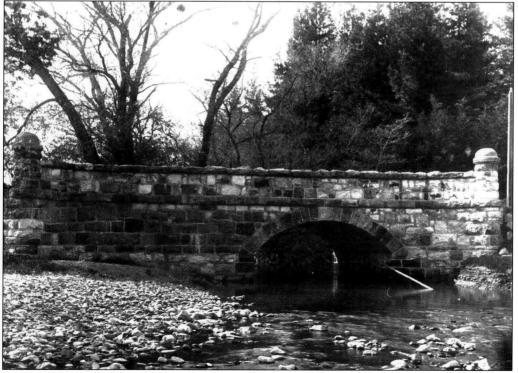

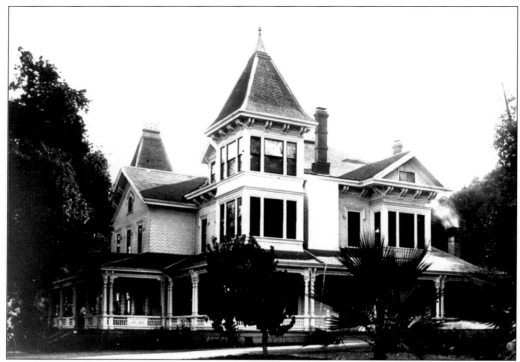

Maplewood was one of the fine mansions along the county road between St. Helena and Calistoga. The Shamp family lived there in the 1870s and made wine.

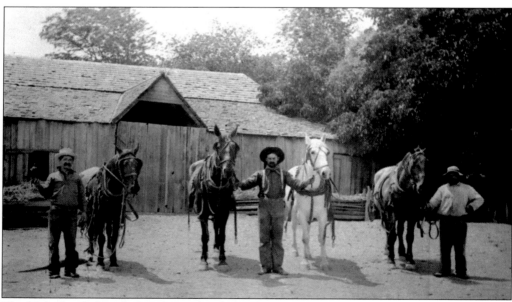

The Holji family bought Maplewood and raised cattle as well as grapes. These cowboys helped keep the herd in order. The one on the left may be holding a jug of wine. In 1944 a pioneer of the 20th century wine industry, Charles Forni, nephew of Tychson Winery founder Antonio Forni, bought Maplewood.

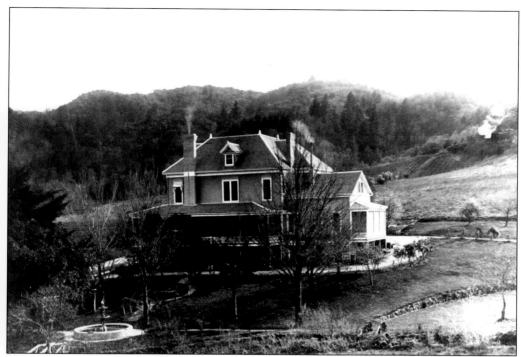

Brookside was an elegant estate near Calistoga, seen here on a winter morning

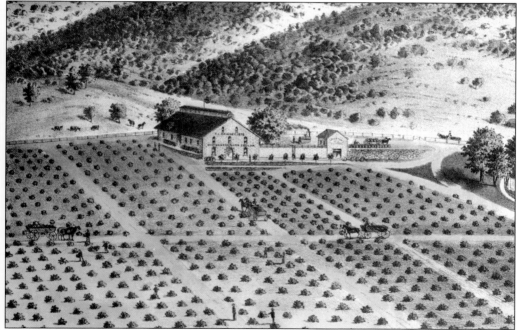

Some who were not rich (but very much wanted to be) borrowed heavily to build and operate their wineries. Terrell Grigsby's Occidental Winery, combined with an ill-fated silver mine, brought its owner financial ruin.

An 1895 map shows who owned the land around St. Helena. The black-and-white diagonal line is the Southern Pacific Railroad. The Napa River, more or less parallels it slightly to the east. The County Road (now Highway 29) also parallels it to the west. Those known to have vineyards and/or wineries at some point in time include:

Row 1: Schram, Shamp, Hitchcock, Tucker, Chaix, Caramello, Rossi, Hall & Tubbs, Lyman

Row 2: Hitchcock, Bourn, Lyman, Trumpler, Laurent, Chabot, Hall & Tubbs

Row 3: Hunt & Carver, Rosenbaum, Tychson, Lyman, Beers, Ehlers, Weinberger, Moffitt, York, Hall & Tubbs

Row 4: Hunt, Chevalier, Beringer, Rosenbaum, Weinberger, Moffitt, Carpy, Laurent, Castner, Merriam, Martinelli, Zange, Snowball, Howell, Carver

Row 5: Hunt, Beringer, Parrott, Kraft, Rossi, Tosetti, Crane, Watt, Lazarus, Mills Kraft, Schoenwald, Crane, Fountain, Mills, McPike, Dowdell, Wheeler

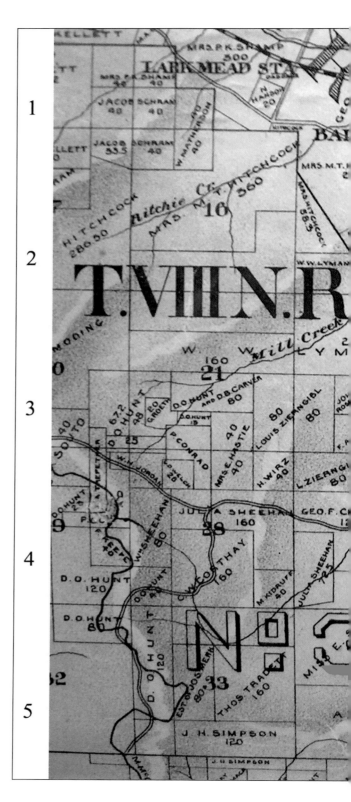

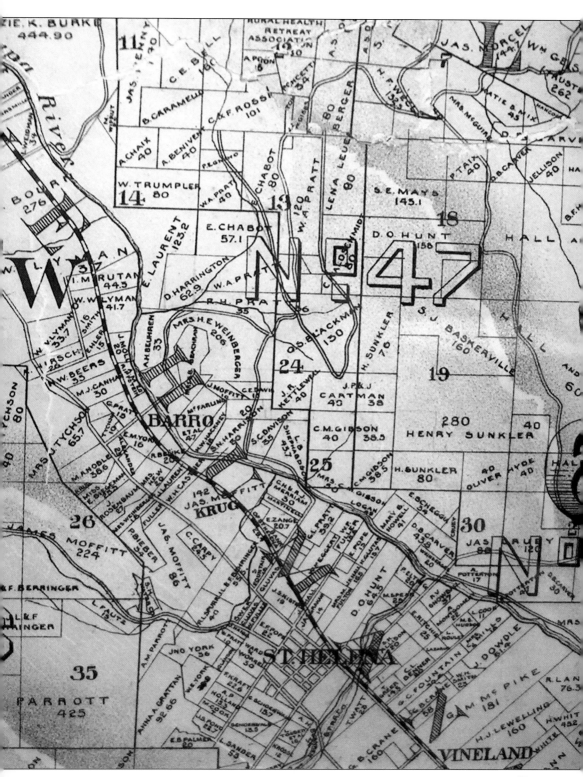

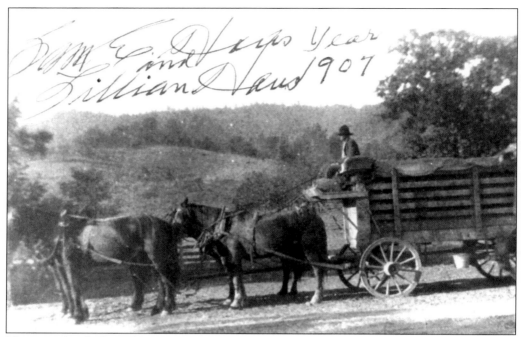

The Haus family farmed in Pope Valley. Bringing produce to market or grapes to crush required a long, winding trip down Howell Mountain. The picture appears to have been taken in 1907.

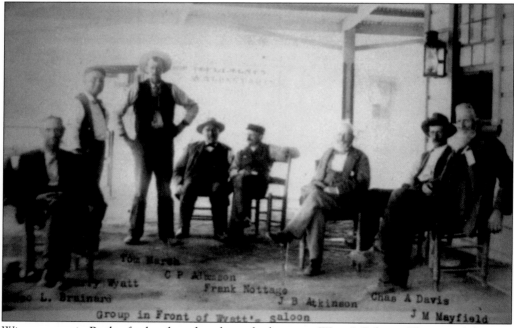

Winegrowers in Rutherford gathered to shoot the breeze at Wyatt's Saloon. Christian Adamson (fourth from left) died in the 1918 influenza epidemic. J.B. Atkinson (third from right) partnered with Seneca Ewer in a winery and lived in a home that is now on the property of the St. Supery Winery. (Courtesy of John York.)

Five

BOOM TIMES

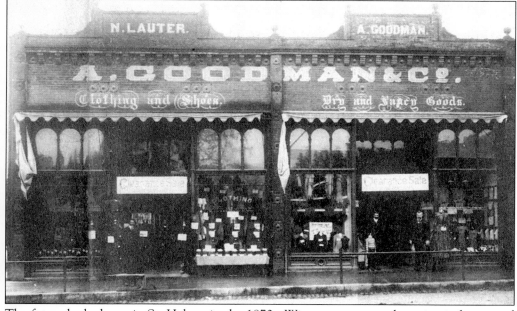

The future looked rosy in St. Helena in the 1870s. Wine was an up-and-coming industry, and mining was also profitable. There was lots of competition in St. Helena for the customer's dollar. Dry goods merchant Abraham Goodman was one of several Jewish shopkeepers who arrived in town in the 1870s. The business he and Nathan Lauter started is still going strong, although its location has changed. Goodman and Lauter supplied mounting blocks and hitching posts for their customers' convenience. Most of the merchants advertised in the *St. Helena Star*. Some touted better quality, others lower prices, and still others a greater selection. The presence of so many stores meant that the local economy was good.

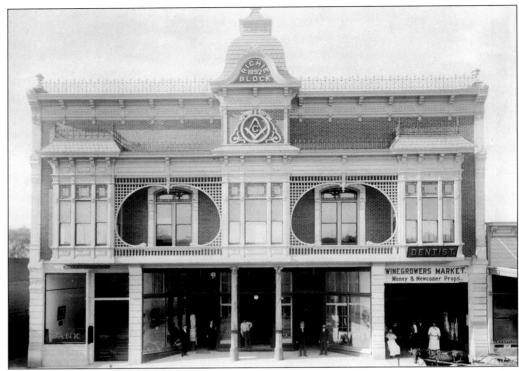

A.N. Bell stands in front of D.B. Carver's grocery and dry goods Store (*right*) where he worked after Carver built it in 1879. Carver bought and sold land all around St. Helena, profiting greatly from the vineyard-planting craze. He even had his own bank. Townsend and Anderson bought the building from Carver in 1881. In 1883 they sold it to the Greenfield brothers, who sold it to A.N. Bell and his brother in 1887. The Bell Brothers moved their store to the Ritchie Building (*above*), which was completed in 1892 and was a great source of pride to the community. John Money created the curving latticework on the second floor. The business on the left is the Savings Bank of St. Helena. Bell Brothers is in the center, and a butcher shop, Money & Newcomer, is on the right. Note the garland on the horse's head (*above, lower right corner*).

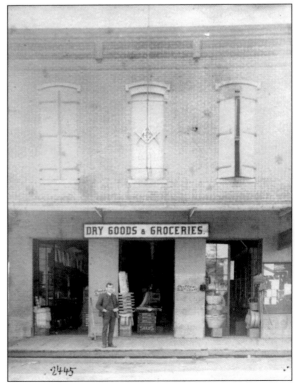

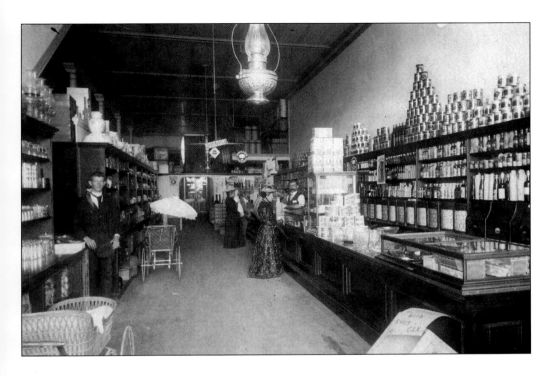

The new Bell Brothers store boasted a grocery store on one side (*above*) and a dry goods store on the other (*below*).

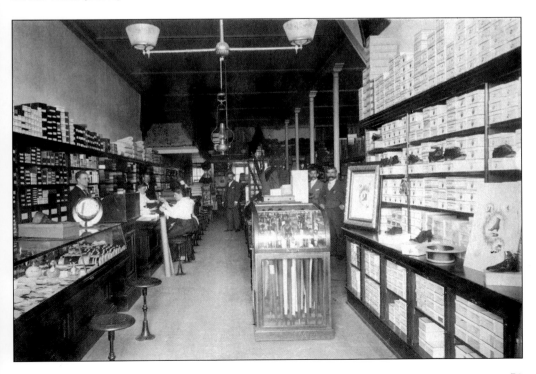

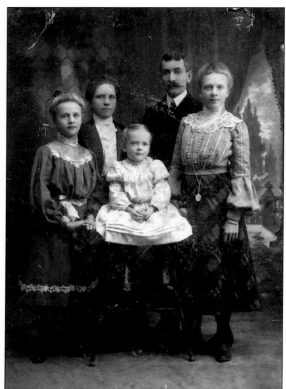

A.N. Bell married the belle of St. Helena, Dixie Chiles. Dixie's father, Joe Chiles, was a pioneer who had been given a Mexican land grant by General Vallejo in 1843. Chiles moved to St. Helena from Rutherford in the 1870s and raised mules. His home was on Spring Street at the site of what is now the Native Sons of the Golden West hall. Seen here, from left to right, are Dixie Alberta Bell, Dixie Chiles Bell, A.N. Bell, Linda May Bell, and, in front, Georgia Bell.

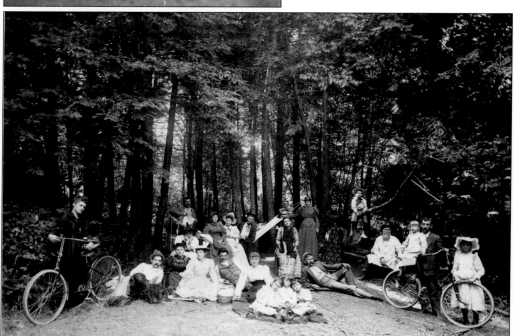

Friends and family of A.N. Bell enjoy an outing in the redwoods. Some may have peddled there on their bicycles.

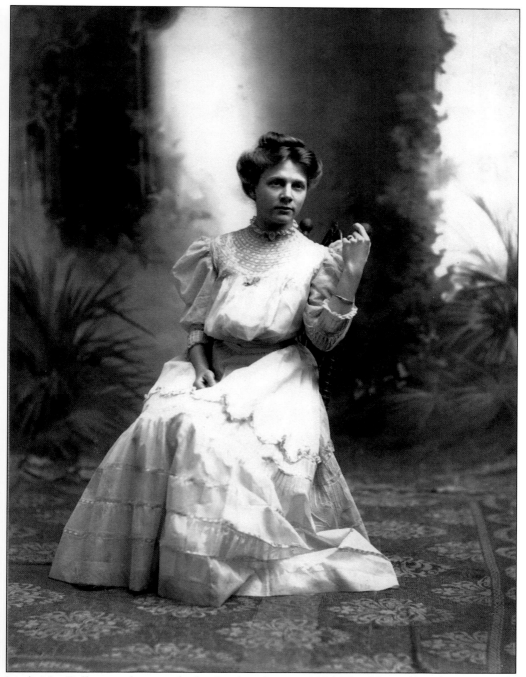

Linda May Bell was a charming high school graduate in 1906. The fabric of her dress was made of sifting, or "bolting," cloth from her grandfather's flourmill in Chiles Valley. The lace survived the San Francisco earthquake and fire.

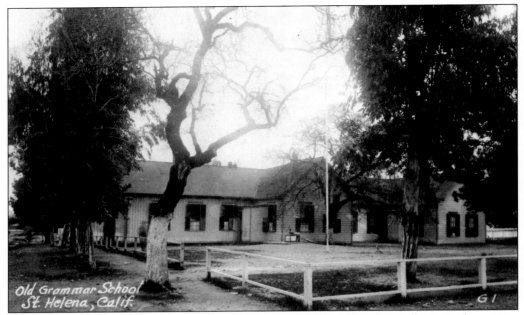

St. Helena's original grammar school had no heat, so children had to bundle up in the winter. The building was auctioned off in three pieces around 1900.

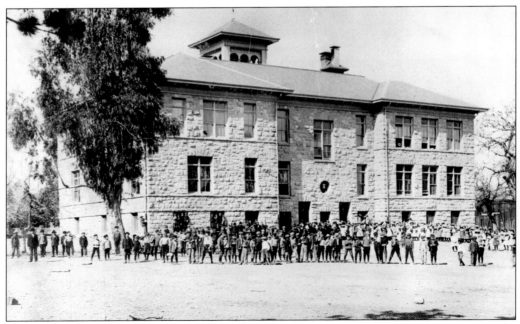

The original grammar school's replacement, seen here in 1907, may have been warmer. The boys are lined up in the front, the girls in the back.

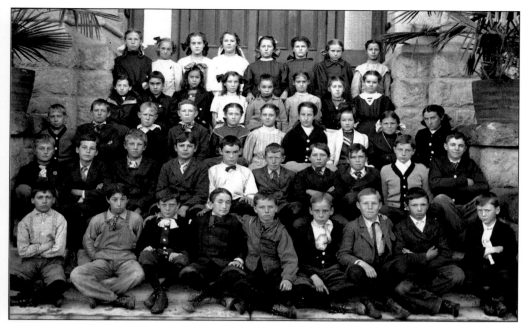

This group of children is similarly arranged, boys in front, girls in back. The undated photo is from the private collection of the Learned family. (Courtesy of Sandra Learned Perry.)

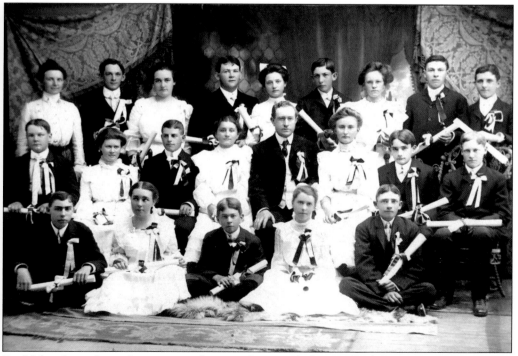

St. Helena's sixth graders receive their graduation diplomas. Diplomas were incentives to encourage children to stay in school. Few of the youngsters here would graduate from high school; college attendance was exceptional.

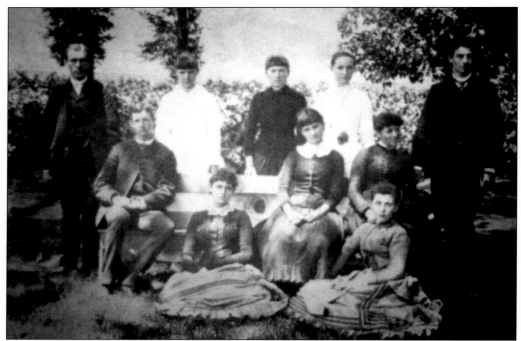

St. Helena High School's graduating class of 1887 was unusual for its preponderance of girls. From left to right are (bottom row) Lillie Bussenius and Miriam Gardner; (middle row) Joe Graham, Lolita Krug, and Anna Kohler; (top row) John T. York, Clara J. York, Frances Cantolena, Sarah Haire, and Ashley Tabor. (Courtesy of John York).

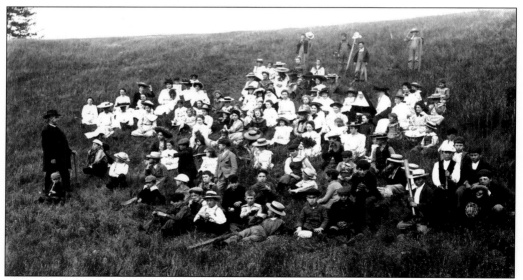

Many Catholic children attended Elmhurst Academy, a private school located just north of town, currently the site of the Seventh-day Adventist church. Four farm children seem to have come to observe the nattily dressed youngsters, and perhaps to watch the baseball game that would soon take place. Note the catcher, crouched with his glove and mask on the lower right, and the boy in the sombrero left of center.

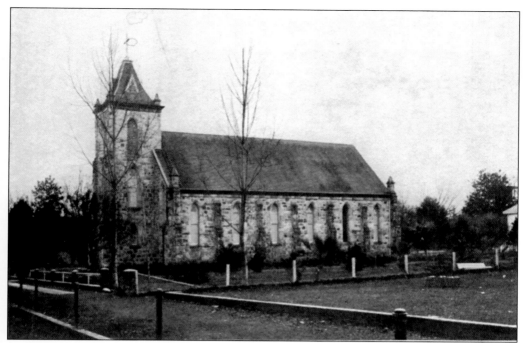

St. Helena's Catholics built a large stone church with a steeple. The steeple burned down in the mid 20th century, but the rest of the edifice was spared.

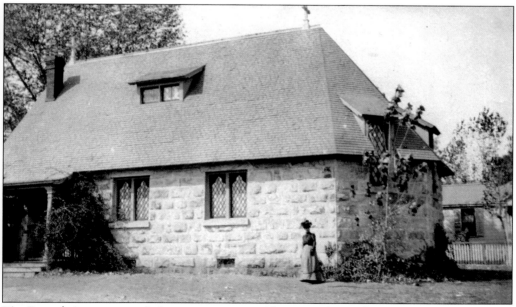

The Episcopalians, many of whom were quite wealthy, wanted something warmer than the drafty old Catholic chapel they had purchased in the 1860s. They sold it to a Mrs. Taylor, who hauled it to Main Street, where it became a saloon. The Episcopalians then hired a Boston architect to design a new church for them, shown here. Originally called Grace Memorial Church, the small, oval stone building was intended to be the center of a much bigger, cross-shaped structure.

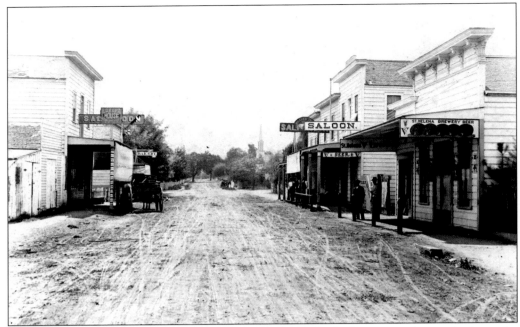

Seen here from its intersection with Main, Spring Street had a brewery and several saloons for those who needed to celebrate or drown their sorrows. Churches were further up the street. (Courtesy of the St. Helena Public Library.)

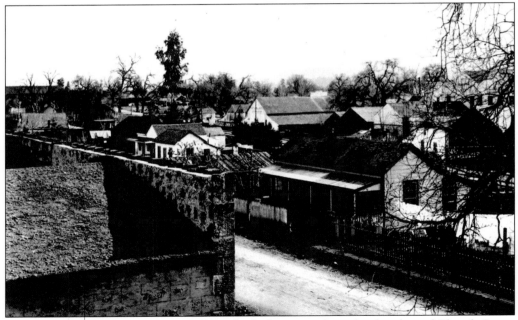

Amateur photographer Henry Lewelling climbed on a roof to take this shot of Church Street in winter. Laundry is drying on the line to the right, and the Southern Pacific railroad tracks pass through backyards. Lewelling, intrigued with all forms of technology, also built a steam-powered automobile. (Courtesy of the St. Helena Public Library.)

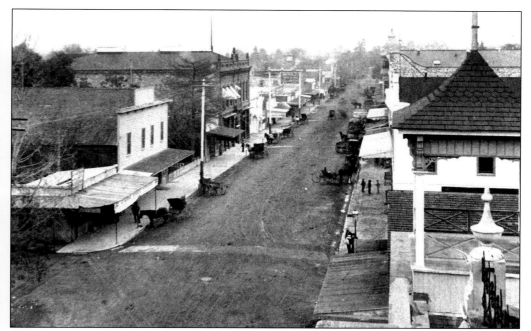

The photographer climbed on a rooftop to memorialize this scene of St. Helena. An obstruction of some kind appears to be blocking the western entrance to Adams Street (ramp to right in foreground). (Courtesy of the St. Helena Public Library.)

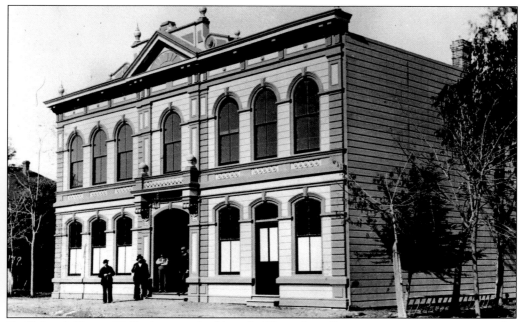

St. Helena's Turner Hall, photographed here by Henry Lewelling, was an enormous asset to the community. Originally built as a venue for athletic competition, the name derived from the German *turn verein*, or sports club. Turner Hall provided space for social events and was even used as a school. (Courtesy of the St. Helena Public Library.)

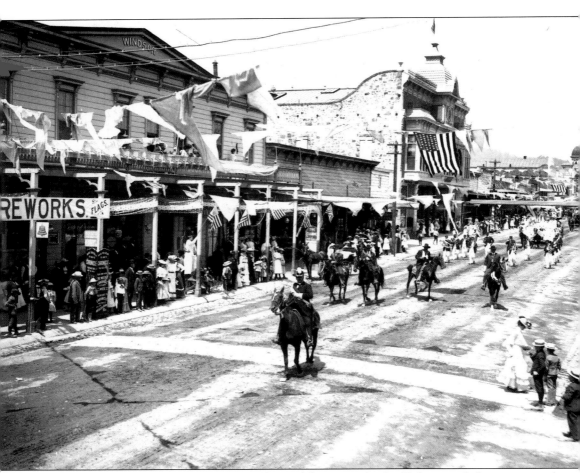

The Fourth of July meant flags, fireworks, and festivities for St. Helena, and the townspeople never tired of parades. Patrons of the Windsor Hotel watch from the balcony.

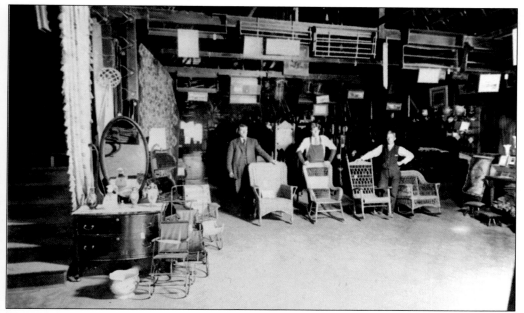

Mercier's Furniture Store occupied the Noble-Galleron Building at 1200 Main Street, St. Helen. Seen here, from left to right, are Mr. Mercier, Ira Humphrey, and Carl Klubescheidt.

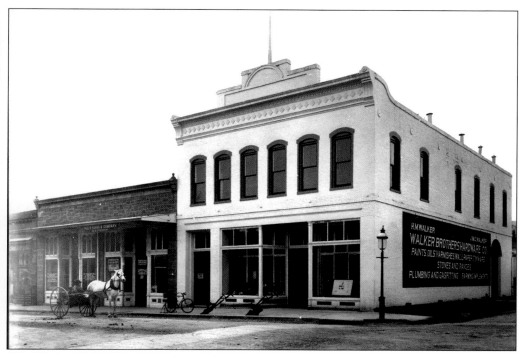

The Kettlewell Building on the southwest corner of Main and Adams Streets once housed a hardware store, although the store didn't stay in business for very long. The white paint has long since faded, and the arched entrance (far right) has been bricked over. The advertisement on the side of the building is illegible now.

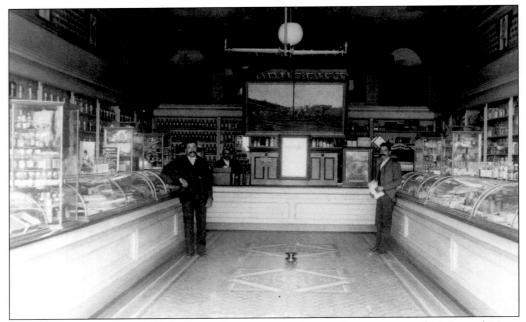

George A. Riggins's Wonderful Drug Store was on the northeast corner of Main and Hunt Streets. George's son Clarence, who became district attorney, may be the young man on the right. Riggins sank a gold monogram, G.A.R., in the cement sidewalk in front of his business. It upset many of the locals because the acronym also stood for Grand Army of the Republic, the Northern army in the Civil War. Many St. Helenans, sympathetic to the Confederacy, were still angry about the war's outcome.

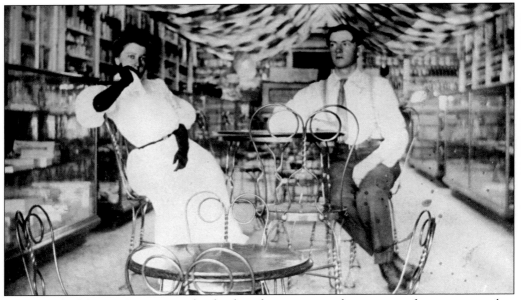

The Wonderful Drug Store was a dandy place for young people to enjoy a fountain treat, but the young woman in long gloves might have been a tad overdressed when this photo was taken in 1907.

Sophie Zierngibl was a paragon of St. Helena millinery fashion in 1908.

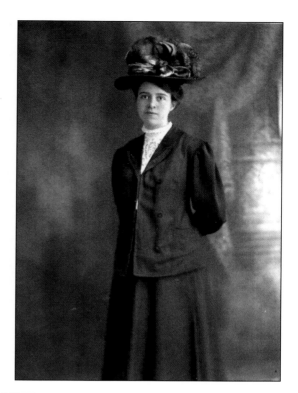

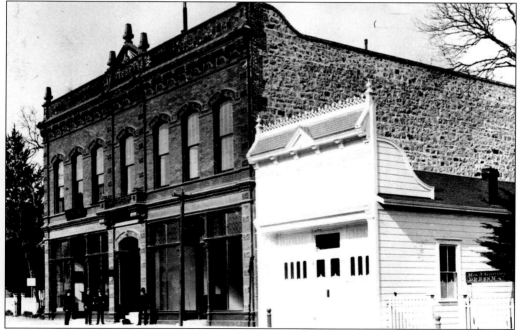

Mrs. J. Gottleib, a dressmaker, did business in this attractive white building next to the Odd Fellows Hall. Some believe that the building had previously served as the business house of a Mrs. Turner, and before that as the Episcopal church and the Catholic chapel.

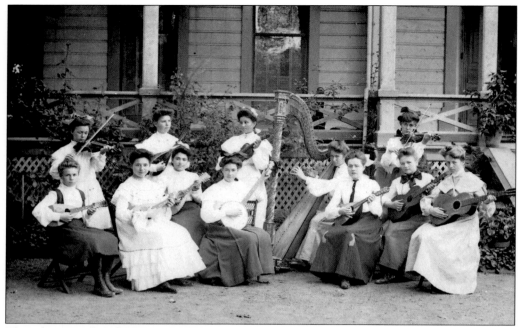

This photograph, taken August 27, 1904, once belonged to Josephine Forni, who may have been in it. She was a student at Elmhurst Academy. Before the days of radio teenagers had to make their own music.

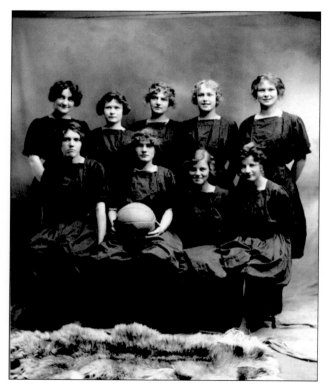

The St. Helena girls' basketball team was often victorious. Front row cagers are Helena Tepping, Alice Taplin (Thorsen), Edith Guigni (Spencer), and Mary Tamagne. The players in the back row are Alice Erickson, Margaret Griffith, Mabel Taplin (Anderson), Josephine Parker, and Lily Nelson (Lewelling).

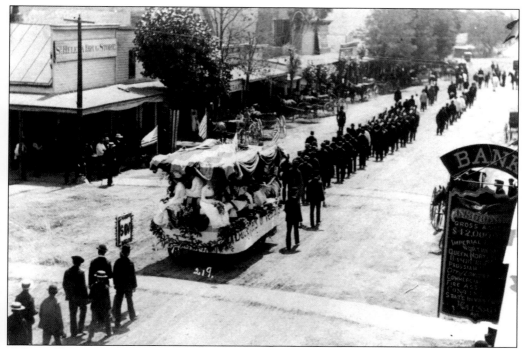

A Sons of Veterans contingent is moving into view (bottom left) in this 1905 parade. Preceding them are veterans of the Spanish-American, Civil, and possibly Mexican-American Wars. A float carries the veterans' daughters.

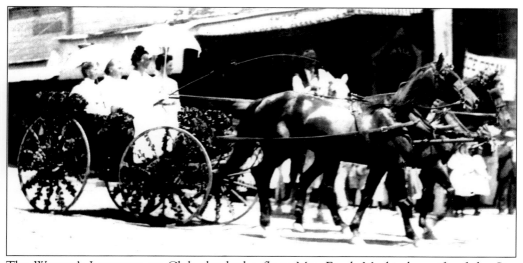

The Women's Improvement Club also had a float. Mrs. Frank Mackinder, wife of the *Star* newspaper editor, founded the organization's St. Helena branch in February 1905. From left to right are Mrs. Hannah Weinberger, president; Mrs. Guzweiler, treasurer; Mrs. L. Walker, secretary; and Mrs. Mackinder.

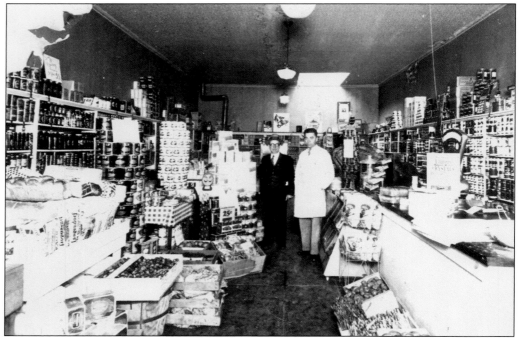

Guigni's in St. Helena was a grocery store in the old tradition. It sold fruits, vegetables, bread, and assorted canned and paper goods. Shoppers went to the butcher for meat, the stationer for paper products, and the tobacconist for cigars.

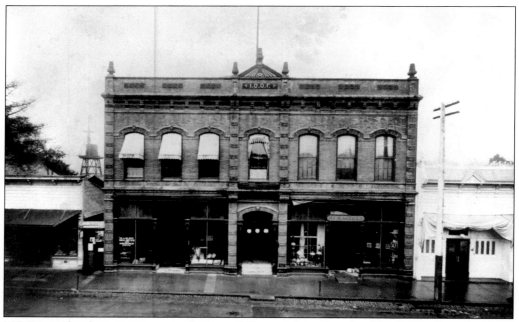

J.H. Steves' hardware store was on the ground floor on the right side of the Odd Fellows Building. W.A. Elgin's real estate and insurance offices were on the left, and a dentist, Dr. Watkins, held forth on the top floor.

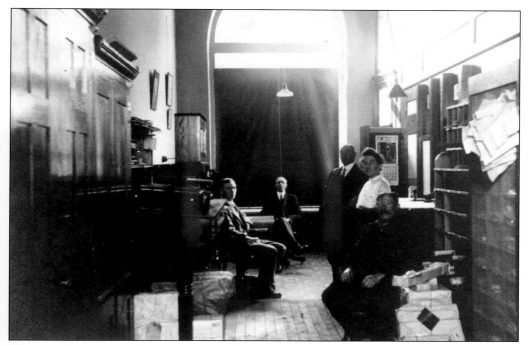

The post office in St. Helena was in the *Star* newspaper building for many years. From left to right are Orville Thompson, assistant postmaster; Frank Mackinder, postmaster (and editor of the *Star*); Theodore Simmonsen, carrier; Louise Klubescheidt, clerk; and Henry Lann, carrier.

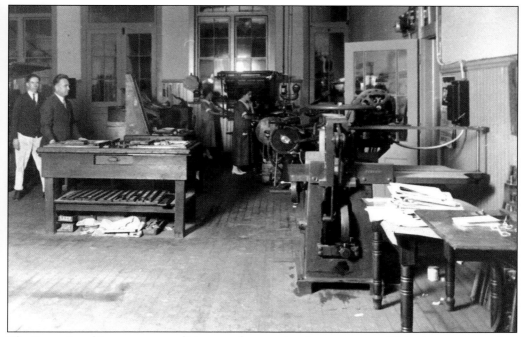

The *Star* printed its newspaper editions on the premises for many years. This photo suggests that the presses sometimes ran late into the night.

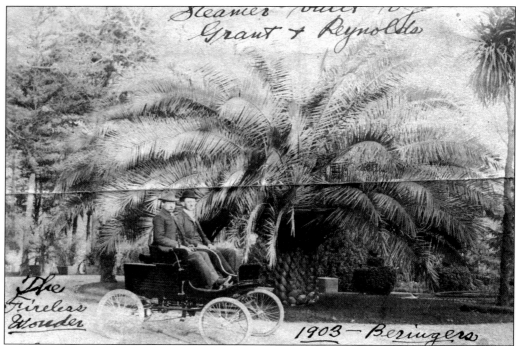

In 1903, John Allison (right) and George Reynolds brought their "Fireless Wonder" to the Beringer Winery. It was a "steamer," powered by hot water, which they built themselves.

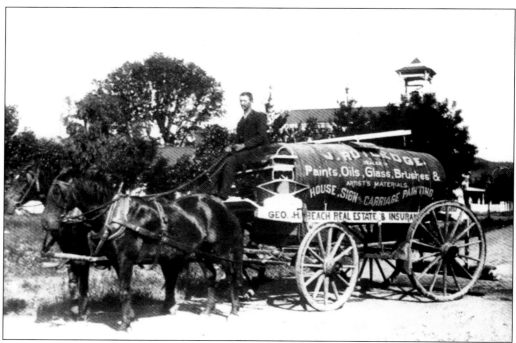

When he wasn't experimenting with high tech mechanics, St. Helenan John Allison ran a water sprayer that kept the dust down on hot summer days. (Courtesy of John York.)

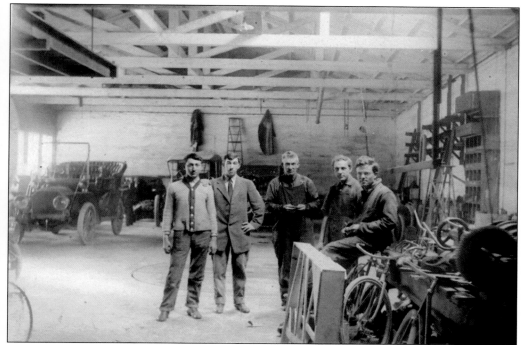

Automotive repair and maintenance were considered high tech, and Philo Grant and his mechanics, pictured here, were well respected in St. Helena. From left to right are Joe Cheli, Earl Mori, Philo Grant, Ad Grigsby, and Ed Bonhote. This building now houses Steve's Hardware.

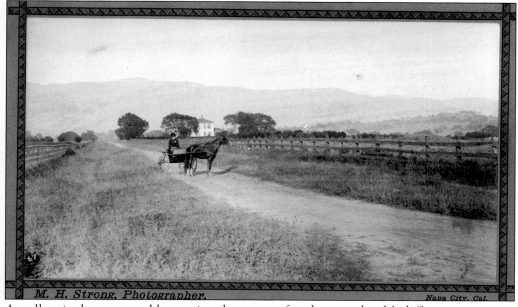

M. H. Strong, Photographer.

Napa City, Cal.

A well-attired woman and her patient horse pose for photographer Mark Strong on a quiet country road. Contraptions like Allison and Reynolds's steamer terrified horses, and often their masters as well.

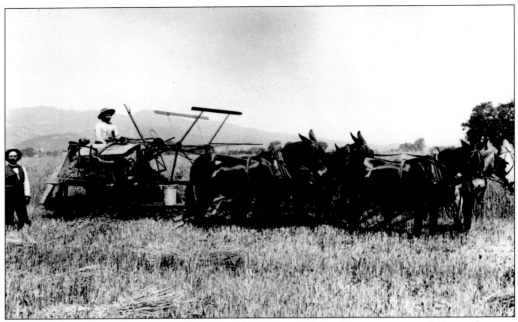

The Lewellings owned an oat field south of St. Helena. Nelce Peterson manned the mule team this June morning in 1892. Growing oats became far less profitable after the invention of the automobile. (Courtesy of the St. Helena Public Library.)

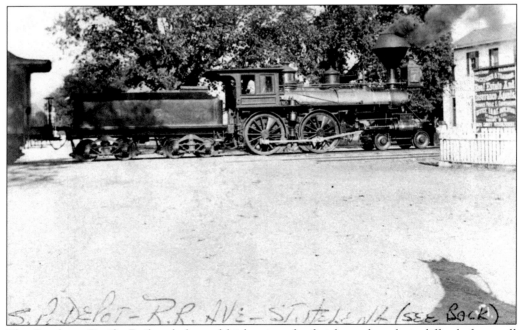

The Southern Pacific Railroad charged high prices for freight and made it difficult for small wineries to make a profit. The railroad also meant less work for horses, symbolically represented by the shadow in the foreground of this shot taken from behind Turner Hall on Railroad Avenue. It wouldn't be long before automobiles turned the railroad into a mere shadow too.

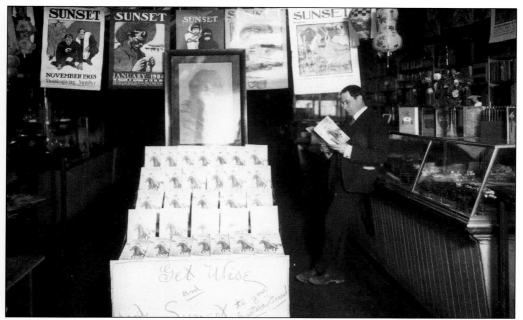

Joe Galewsky sold magazines (he was apparently very fond of *Sunset*), newspapers and books, stationery, school supplies, and a myriad of other paper products. Later he dealt with paper products in a different way, serving as St. Helena's postmaster during both World Wars.

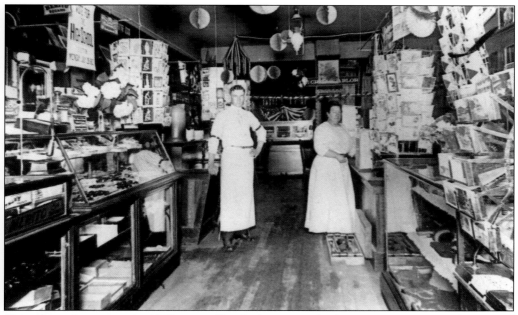

Grauss's variety store in Calistoga offered cigars, candy, ice cream, paper products, and party decorations. Felix Grauss, a Republican, was Calistoga's postmaster until Woodrow Wilson became president (1913) and the appointment went to a Democrat. (Courtesy of the Sharpsteen Museum.).

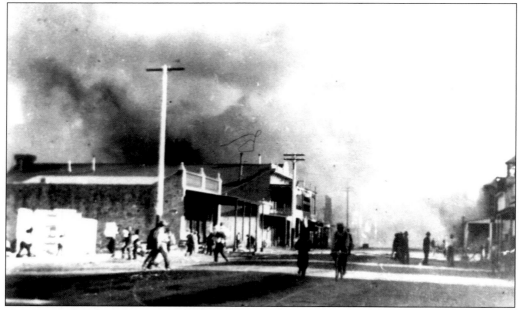

Sam Brannan was not successful in creating the posh resort spa he had envisioned at the head of the Valley, but Calistoga, the town that congealed to support the spa, managed to hang on. A devastating fire in the summer of 1901 burned down most of the buildings there. It started behind John Wolfe's grocery store just after 5 p.m. and spread quickly. (Courtesy of the Sharpsteen Museum.)

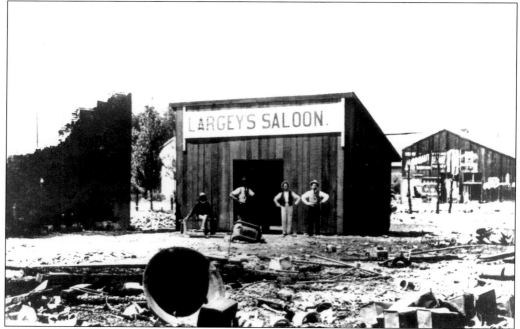

The first building reconstructed after the devastating 1901 Calistoga fire was Ed Largey's saloon. (Courtesy of the Sharpsteen Museum.)

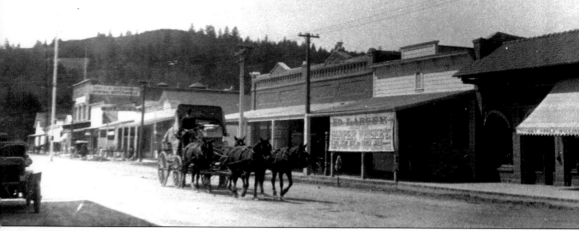

By 1910 Calistoga had fully recovered from the fire, and Largey's saloon was still in business. Motorists from out of town braved the rutted roads to visit the hot springs there. To ensure that no more fires would level the town, the fire department bought a fire engine. Unfortunately the new machine was so expensive that there was no money left in the town coffers for other expenses, like street repairs. A similar event occurred in St. Helena in 1916. Members of the fire department walked off the job because the council refused to buy them a new engine. When the council capitulated and purchased the machine there wasn't enough money left in the treasury to keep the streetlamps lit.

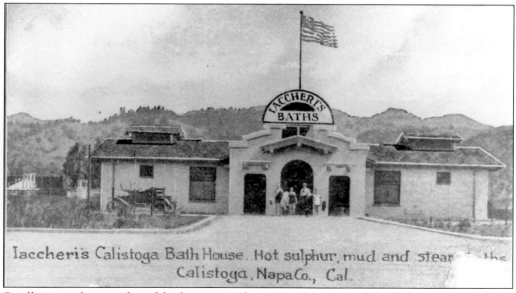

Iaccheri's Calistoga Bath House. Hot sulphur, mud and stear the Calistoga, Napa Co., Cal.

Small, privately owned mud baths remained an important part of the little town's economy. This old postcard advertises Iaacheri's. Note also the antique automobiles. (Courtesy of the Sharpsteen Museum.)

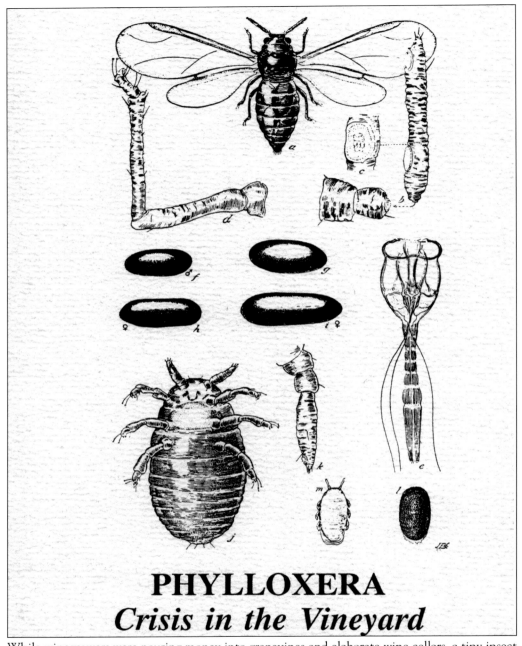

PHYLLOXERA
Crisis in the Vineyard

While winegrowers were pouring money into grapevines and elaborate wine cellars, a tiny insect was there to suck those plants dry. The phylloxera louse, pictured on this modern pamphlet prepared by Randy Murphy for the Napa Valley Museum, was a tiny creature that sported different shapes during its life cycle. It had worked out a relatively peaceful co-existence with native mission grapes, which were immune to its secretions. It was poisonous, however, to European grape stock, the kind vintners favored for the excellent wine they produced. The phylloxera bug fed on the tender tips of the vines' roots, which caused swellings to bulge around the insect's body. These galls choked off the supply of nutrients to the plant and eventually killed it.

Six

HARD TIMES

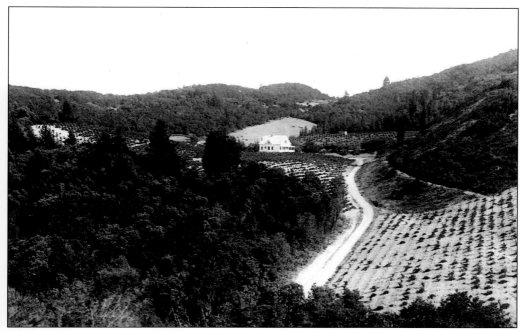

These vineyards in the western hills, photographed in 1904, were infested with phylloxera, as were virtually all the other vines in Napa County. (Courtesy of the Michael Yates family.)

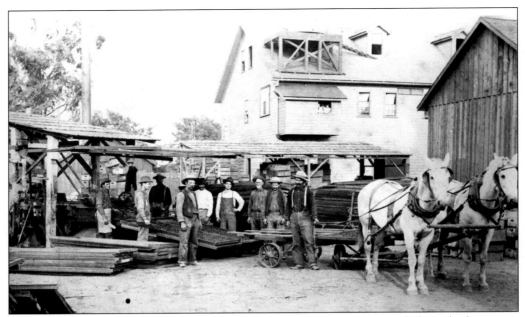

After the phylloxera scourge many farmers pulled out their grapevines and planted other crops. Prunes and walnuts were the most common replacements. Here farm workers load racks of dried prunes for shipment to the packer.

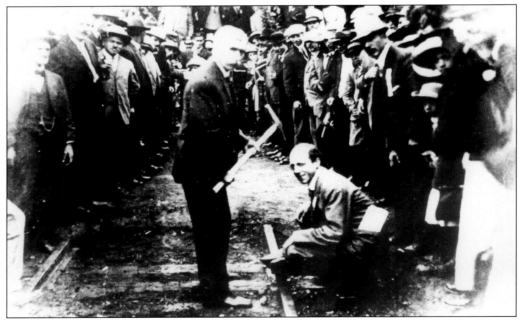

Mainly due to problems in the wine industry, the towns of the Napa Valley did not grow as quickly as those in other Bay Area counties. To stimulate the local economy, the county supervisors permitted a developer to install an electric railroad. The line ran from Vallejo to Calistoga and was powered by overhead wires. Here, dignitaries drive in the last spike for the new electric railroad at its terminus in Calistoga.

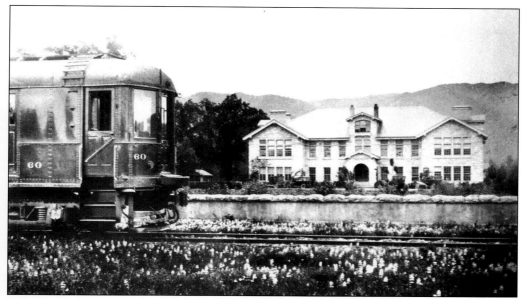

Called an "interurban railroad," the Vallejo, Benicia & Napa Valley Railroad was a combination trolley and train. Although it was inexpensive to ride, it posed serious hazards. People walking on the tracks were sometimes electrocuted, especially after rainstorms. The train occasionally jumped the tracks, and the wires that ran the length of the Valley were unsightly. Here it passes St. Helena High School, which later became known as Vintage Hall, the first home of the Napa Valley Museum.

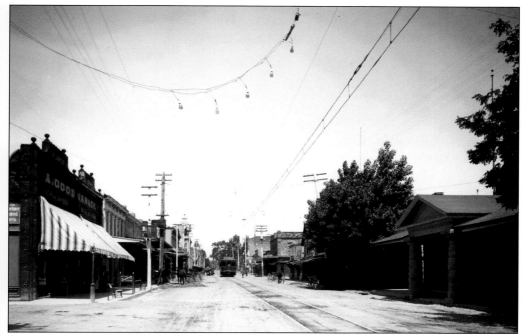

Like the Southern Pacific, the VB & NVRR (Vallejo, Benicia & Napa Valley Railroad) had many stops. One was in the center of St. Helena.

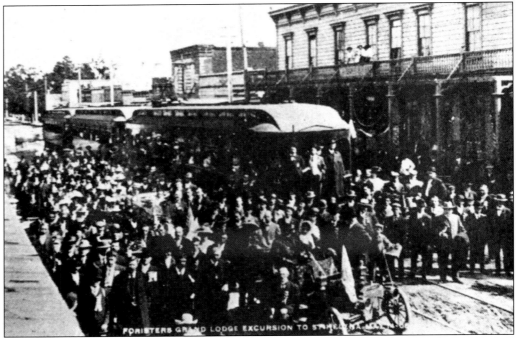

In 1908, the electric railroad filled three cars with Foresters, members of a fraternal organization, and shuttled them to St. Helena. Merchants considered their arrival a great boon, because the local economy was suffering. Many people had moved away because of the drop in the region's industry and agriculture.

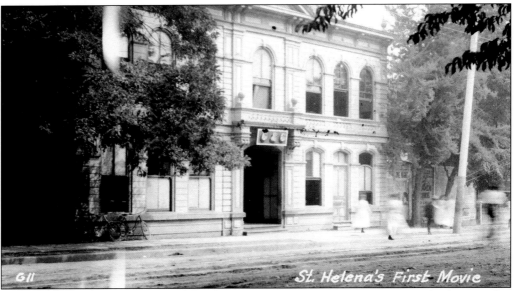

Turner Hall was the site of St. Helena's first movie theater, the G & G, but the big wooden building did not age well and was eventually torn down. The Lyman family bought the land and donated it to the City of St. Helena for use as a park.

Charles Krug invested everything in the wine business and lost it. A drop in the national economy and the phylloxera epidemic, combined with naïve business practices, caused him to declare bankruptcy. After his death, his brother-in-law and general manager Louis Bruck took over the business. Louis's son Bismarck (people called him Mark) succeeded his father as general manager. Bismarck Bruck, shown here, was friendly, intelligent, and a strong asset to the Napa Valley. (Courtesy of Kergan Bruck)

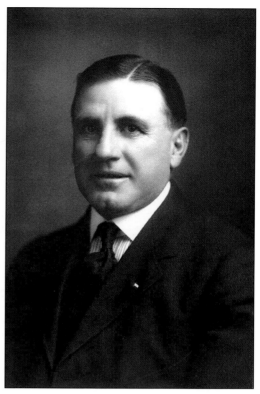

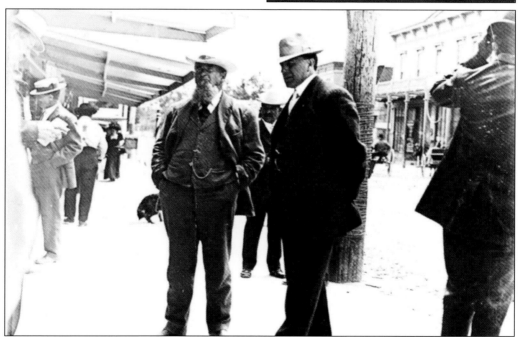

Pioneer winemaker Henry Pellet and Bismarck Bruck, general manager of Charles Krug Winery, have a chat.

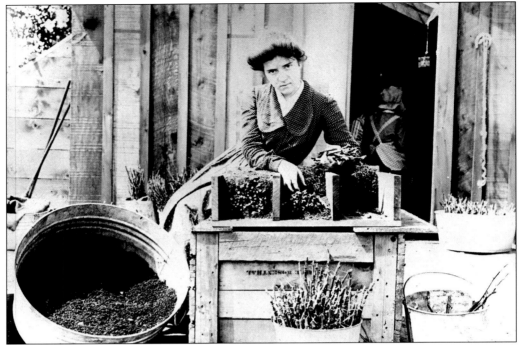

Bruck was among those who advocated grafting European wine varietals onto the rootstock of native vines that were resistant to phylloxera. It worked, and the industry was saved—for a while. Here, a vineyard worker is sorting rootstock.

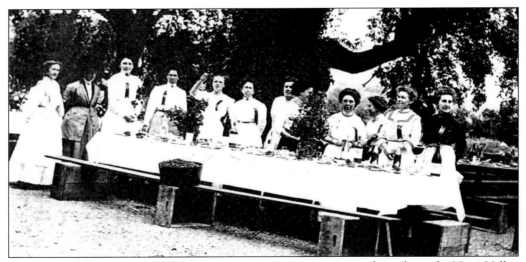

The Women's Improvement Club was a very important civic group throughout the Napa Valley and is still active today. The women shown in this August 10, 1910 picture at Crane Park are all wearing ribbons, having perhaps won awards. From left to right are Miss Mary Shepard, Mrs. Hannah Weinberger, Mrs. F.C. Newton, Mrs. Anderson, Mrs. Murray, Mrs. W.B. Bell, Mrs. Bismarck Bruck (president), Mrs. Leslie Stern, Mrs. Walter Metzner, Mrs. Cooper, Mrs. Frank Alexander, and Mrs. Philo Grant. The St. Helena Women's Improvement Club was scolded by other women's clubs for serving wine at club functions.

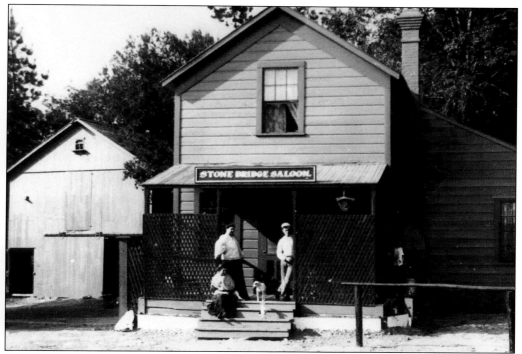

The Stone Bridge Saloon was St. Helena's most notorious house of ill repute. The proprietress, Mary Selowski, spent time behind bars—for serving liquor without a license. Public sentiment against alcohol consumption rose sharply in the years leading up to World War I.

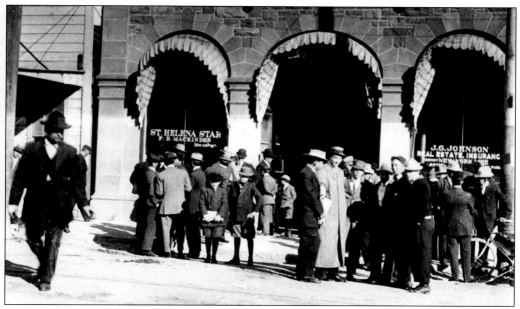

Men and boys wait outside the office of the *St. Helena Star* in 1911. Women and girls were discouraged from taking too much interest in news outside the home. Perhaps it was thought to be too upsetting.

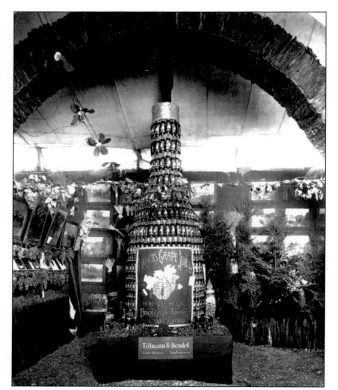

Aware of the public's disaffection with alcoholic beverages, Bismarck Bruck produced unfermented grape juice at Bruckwine (Charles Krug Winery) with premium grapes from the Moffitt vineyard near St. Helena. His non-alcoholic grape juice was featured at the Panama-Pacific Exposition in 1915. (Courtesy of Kergan Bruck.)

The Volstead Act, also known as Prohibition, ended the Napa Valley's wine industry in 1920. Most expected the dry times to last a year or two at most, but as it dragged on bootlegging became a thriving cottage industry. This winemaking family of the 1920s may be toasting the good old days—illegally.

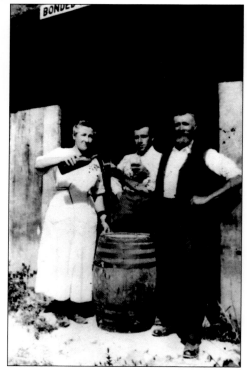

St. Helena's Theodore Bell (no relation to A.N. Bell) was Napa County's youngest district attorney, a U.S. Congressman, and three-time Democratic candidate for governor. A stalwart champion of the wine industry, he challenged the Volstead Act in court. He lost. His vigorous anti-Prohibition position won him many enemies. He was killed in 1922 when his car was forced off the road on a lonely stretch of highway in Bolinas. The other driver was never caught, and many believed it was no accident. (Courtesy of the California State Library)

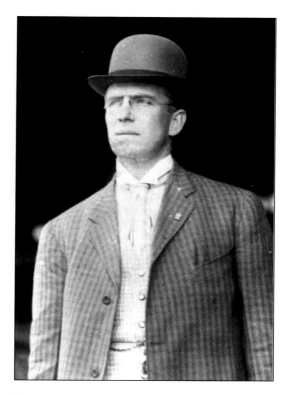

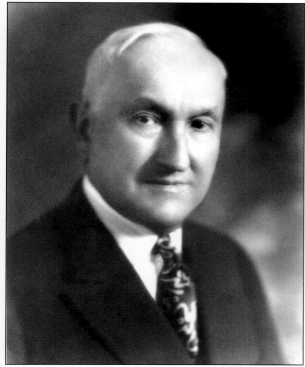

The only wineries to remain open after Prohibition was enacted were those making sacramental wine. Georges de Latour, scion of a French winemaking family, bought the Ewer-Atkinson winery in 1915 and secured contracts to provide altar wine for the Catholic Church. He called his winery "Beaulieu," beautiful place. (Courtesy of the Beaulieu Winery.)

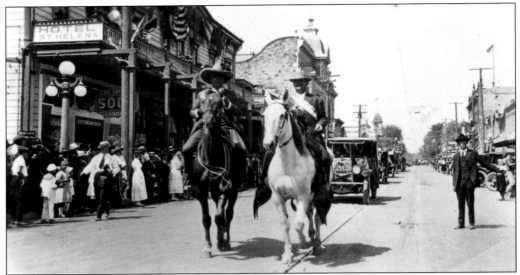

Bootleggers abounded in the Napa Valley during Prohibition. Events like the annual Fourth of July parade attracted thousands of folks from out of town who used the occasion to stock up on illegal beverages. The man on the white horse is John McCormick, a life-long St. Helenan from a pioneering family. (Courtesy of Sandra Learned Perry.)

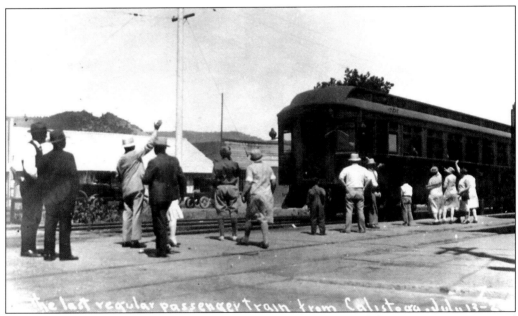

The stock market crash of 1929 put an end to the good times of the Roaring Twenties and thrust the final dagger into the wine industry. Tourists no longer came to the Valley to fill their suitcases with bottles of brandy or bootleg wine, triggering the Southern Pacific to cut passenger service to Calistoga. This photo shows the last train leaving the station. (Courtesy of the Sharpsteen Museum.)

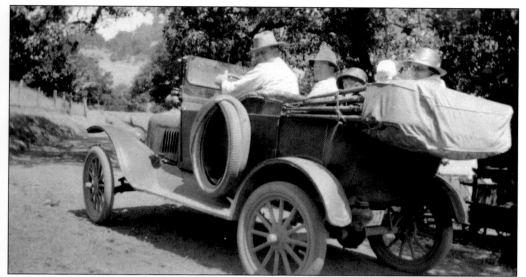

Hard times meant simple pleasures, like drives in the country with family and friends. On this outing in the hills John McCormick and his family are wise to have brought spare tires. (Courtesy of Sandra Learned Perry.)

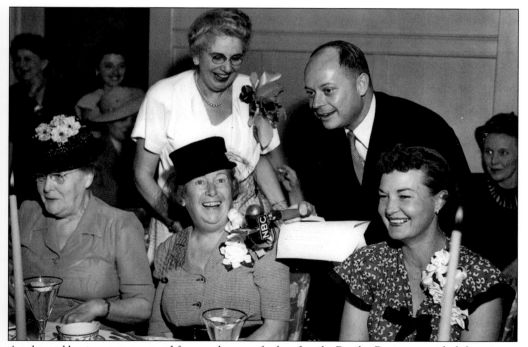

A talented businesswoman and fierce advocate for her family, Bertha Beringer guided the winery through the lean years of Prohibition. Beringer Winery made sacramental wine, marketed bricks of dried wine grapes for home winemaking, and sold off parcels of land to keep the winery solvent. When Prohibiton was finally repealed, Bertha sought public relations opportunities. Seated fom left to right at this NBC Radio airing are Ethel Beringer, Bertha Beringer, and Nita Abruzzini. (Courtesy of Sandra Learned Perry.)

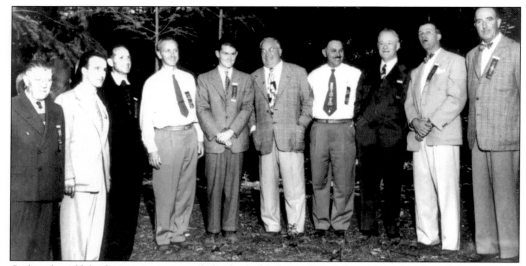

Only a handful of wineries survived the bad old days of Prohibition, and only a few new ones were in operation before1950. Industry leaders meet at the Bourn estate on Sulphur Springs Avenue in St. Helena in 1949. From left to right are Charles Forni (Napa Valley Co-Op), Robert Mondavi (Charles Krug), Brother Timothy (Christian Brothers), unknown, Michael Ahern (Freemark Abbey), Charlie Beringer (Beringer Brothers), Fred Abruzzini (Beringer Brothers), Louis M. Martini (Martini Winery), John Daniel (Inglenook), Martin Stelling (wine grower). (Courtesy of Walt and Geri Raymond.)

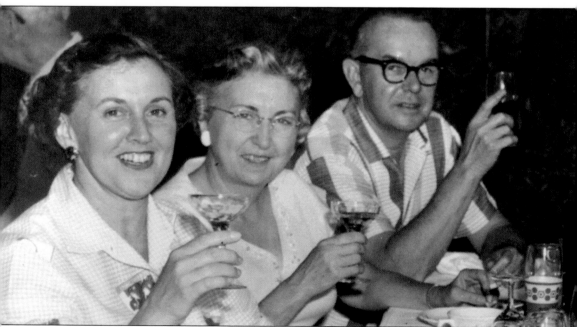

Like the winegrowers almost a century before them, several of the Napa Valley vintners formed a club devoted to eating, drinking wine, and supporting one another in bringing their craft back into the public spotlight. They named their organization the Napa Valley Vintner's Association. The NVVA hosted sumptuous fetes. Seated around the table in this early

To help modernize his winery and the industry as a whole, Georges de Latour convinced a superior European winemaker, Andre Tchelistcheff, to come to the Napa Valley. Tchelistcheff was disturbed by the sorry state of the cellars and equipment and set about improving the quality of the wine. Tchelistcheff mentored many of the people who would become the Valley's most important winemakers including Joe Heitz, Warren Winiarski, Mike Grgich, and a host of others.

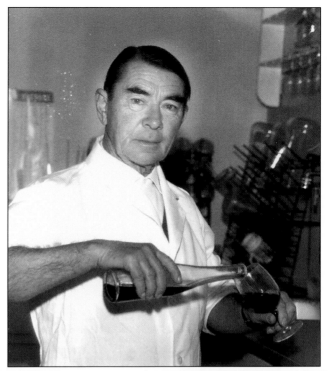

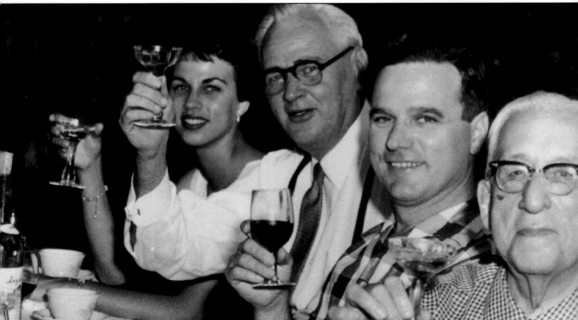

NVVA affair left to right are Blanche Mondavi, Bert Conrey, Harry Conrey (Beaulieu), Otto Gramlow's daughter and Otto Gramlow, Peter Mondavi (Charles Krug) and Carl Bundschu (Inglenook). (Courtesy of Napa Valley Vintner's Association.)

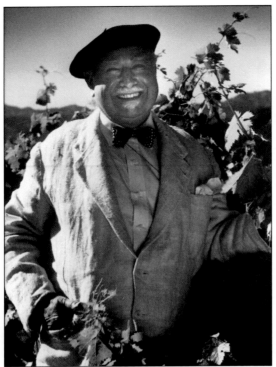

Bon vivant Francis Lewis "Paco" Gould came to the Napa Valley from New York and saw great potential in Napa wines. Carl Bundschu, manager of Inglenook, gave him a tour of the area, and he briefly took a job at Freemark Abbey, the former Forni winery, as an advisor. In 1949 Paco joined C. Mondavi & Sons, the old Krug Winery, and created a public relations department there. He started a periodical called *Bottles and Bins* to stimulate interest and educate wine drinkers.

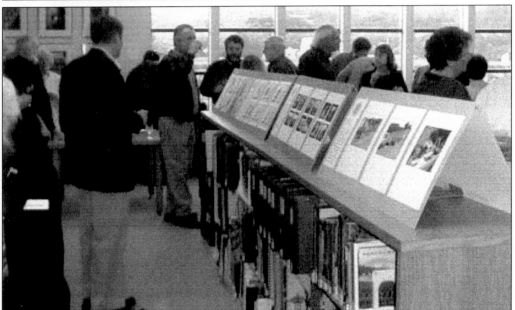

In 1963 Paco Gould, food writer MFK Fisher, and printer James Beard established the Napa Valley Wine Library Association to collect books and other documents about wine and viticulture. The collection, which is part of the St. Helena Public Library, now has more than 3,500 titles and a priceless three-part oral history transcribed from interviews with industry pioneers. (Courtesy of the Napa Valley Wine Library.)

Seven

MODERN TIMES

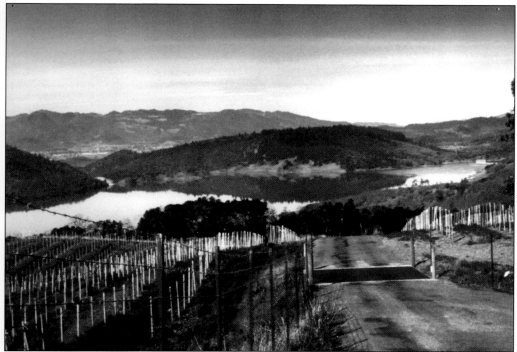

Concerned that developers would build homes and businesses on land that was uniquely suited to viticulture, wine industry supporters passed a law restricting the sale of land outside city limits to parcels of no less than 40 acres. The Williamson Act of 1968 established an agricultural preserve in the Napa Valley. It was a landmark decision, the first of its kind anywhere. Given credibility in a powerful way, the California wine industry exploded. This view was taken from Chappellet vineyards.

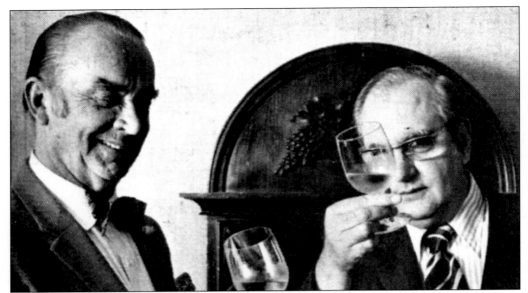

Large food and beverage corporations identified the Napa Valley as a good bargain and began buying up the wineries. United Vintners, part of a vineyard cooperative, purchased Inglenook, which at the time was acceptable to owner John Daniel and his family. But in 1969 a Connecticut company, Heublein, acquired United Vintners and started making jug wine. This may have appealed to novice wine consumers, but it appalled Daniel and many others in the Valley. Within a few months, Heublein also bought Beaulieu. Nestle, a Swiss corporation, acquired the Beringer Winery in 1971. Several other corporations, many of them foreign, scooped up additional wineries. Like United Vintners, the parent corporations themselves were bought and sold. Here, Beringer's new top brass, executives Bob Bras and H. Peter Jurgens, swirl the wine and observe the color. Like the Heublein companies, their game plan was to provide a wide selection of low cost wines.

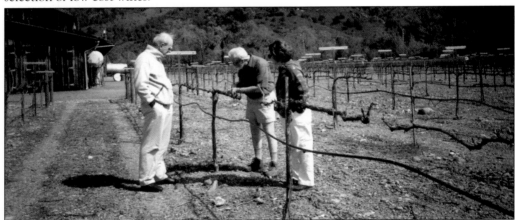

While large corporations bought up Napa wineries, private investors were also discovering the Napa Valley. The troubled 1960s and the even more chaotic 1970s drove many families to seek a quieter, simpler life in a land that seemed immune to modern complexities. With his brother John, San Franciscan Sloan Upton (center) was among many who bought acreage and planted grapes. Their goal was to produce premium grapes for small runs of high quality wine, a game plan diametrically opposed to that of the big corporations.

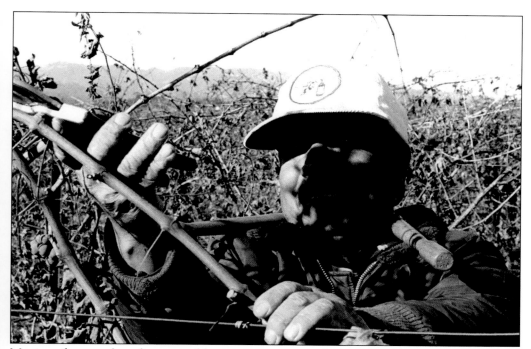

Mexican farm workers first started harvesting grapes in the post-World War II era. It wasn't until the 1970s that a significant influx of Hispanic laborers came to live year-round in the towns and cities of the Napa Valley.

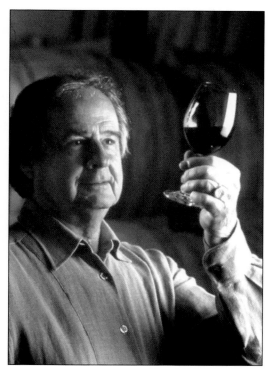

A blind wine tasting held at the Inter-Continental Hotel in Paris in 1976 was another watershed for the Napa Valley wine industry. British wine retailer Steven Spurrier organized it, expecting to promote sales in his Paris shop. Warren Winiarksi's 1973 Stag's Leap Cabernet Sauvignon and Jim Barrett's 1973 Chateau Montelena Chardonnay won first place, astounding the French, embarrassing Spurrier, and impressing enophiles the world over. The Napa vintners rejoiced. Here, Warren Winiarski enjoys a Stag's Leap selection. (Photo by Charles O'Rear; courtesy of Stag's Leap Wine Cellars.)

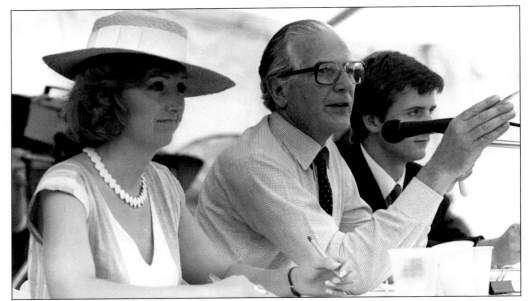

In 1981 the Napa Valley Vintner's Association began hosting an annual auction of wine lots. The net proceeds went to charity. World class auctioneers like Christie's Michael Broadbent (center) emceed the auction. On the left is Shirley Knudsen, who organized the auction in its early years. To date, the auction has garnered more than $300 million for local causes. (Courtesy of the Napa Valley Vintner's Association.)

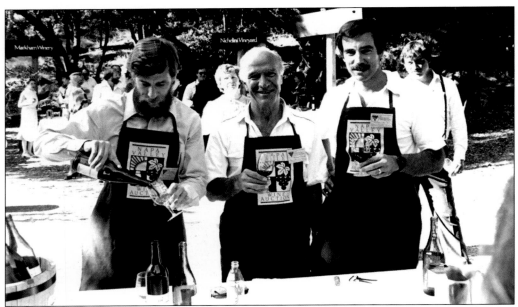

The Mondavi family promoted the Wine Auction from the very beginning. From left to right here are the Mondavis, Timothy, Robert, and Michael. Robert Mondavi introduced Napa Valley wines to the rest of the world. His summer music series, and that of his brother Peter at Charles Krug, helped bring the world to the Napa Valley. (Photo by Jana Russon; courtesy of the Napa Valley Vintner's Association.)

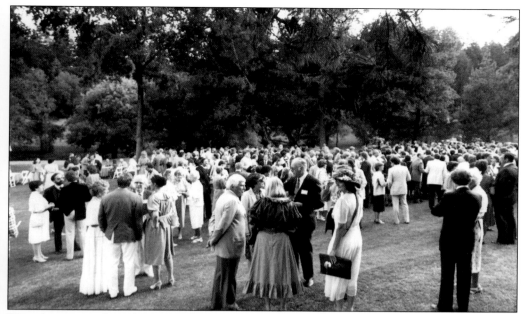

Wine lovers mingle with wine makers at the Meadowood resort, the site of the Wine Auction. (Photo by Jana Russon; courtesy of the Napa Valley Vintner's Association.)

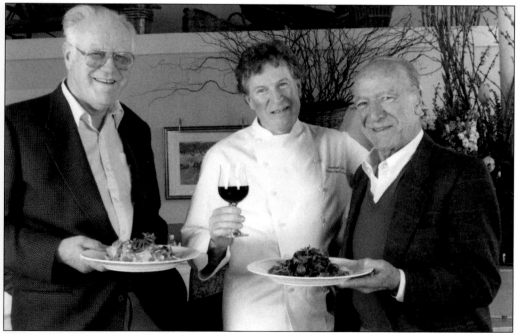

The auction ends with a banquet that pairs great foods with great wines. Entertainment is also provided. At first it was home grown, but as the event grew in popularity, top-notch entertainers were also invited. Here, Louis Martini (Louis M. Martini Winery), Jeremiah Tower (Stars Restaurant), and Robert Mondavi sample each other's wares. (Photo by Jana Russon; courtesy of the Napa Valley Vintner's Association.)

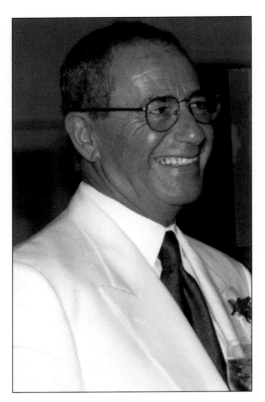

Oddly, the notion of combining great wine with great cuisine was slow in coming to the Napa Valley. Restaurateur Claude Rouas was the first to invest in the construction of a world class Napa Valley eatery. He established Auberge du Soleil in 1981. To provide variety for his customers Claude bought a rundown saloon in Yountville and created the first Piatti restaurant. More first class restaurants followed Rouas's lead. The presence of these restaurants improved the Napa lifestyle, especially in the Up Valley, and the price of land skyrocketed. (Courtesy of Claude Rouas.)

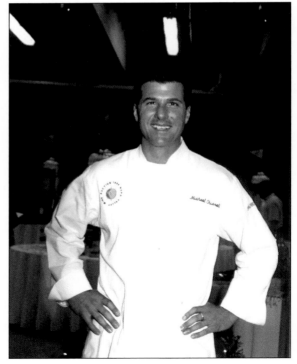

Michael Chiarello is the chef and owner of TraVigne restaurant in St. Helena. (Photo by Jana Russon; courtesy of the Napa Valley Vintner's Association.)

Other top-notch chefs came to the Napa Valley after 1981. Some focused their efforts on preparing food at individual wineries, like Parisian Michel Cornu at Far Niente. (Photo by Jana Russon, courtesy of the Napa Valley Vintner's Association.)

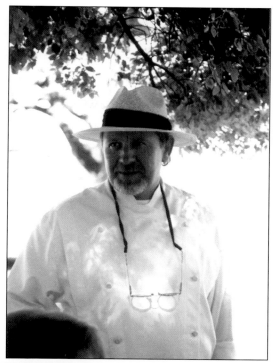

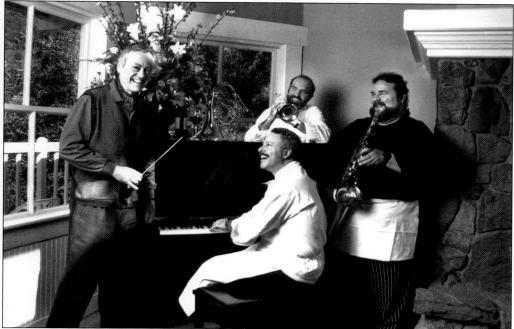

Wine, music, and fine cuisine are all represented in this photograph. From left to right are vintner Agustin Huneeus (Quintessa Winery), Fred Halpert (Brava Terrace), Bob Hurley (Hurley's), and Jan Birnbaum (Catahoula). (Photo by Jana Russon, courtesy of the Napa Valley Vintner's Association.)

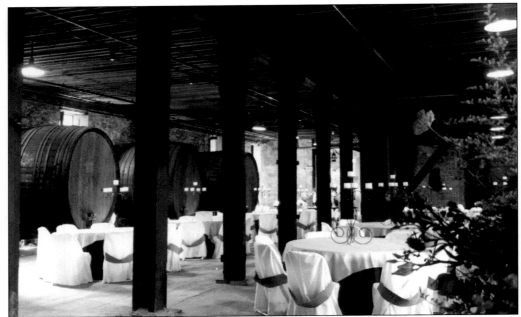

Most wineries host banquets from time to time. Once known as the Christian Brothers Winery, the Culinary Institute of America is now a school for professionals in the food business and lends out its Barrel Room for elegant soirees. (Photo by Jana Russon.; courtesy of Napa Valley Vintner's Association.)

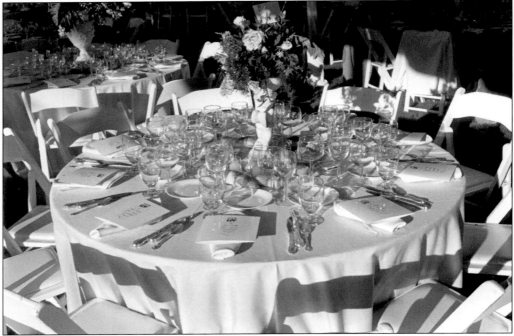

Napa Valley parties often require a major investment in glassware. (Photo by Jana Russon; courtesy of the Napa Valley Vintner's Association.)

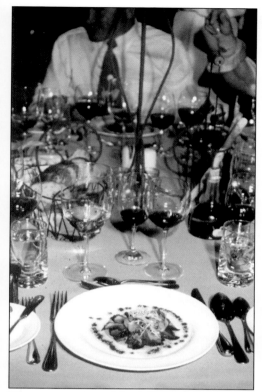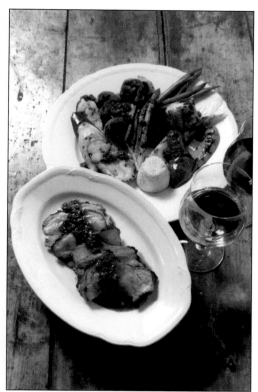

The presentation of food, like the appearance of the wine in the glass, and the label and capsule on the bottle, are all art forms in themselves. (Photos by Jana Russon; courtesy of the Napa Valley Vintner's Association.

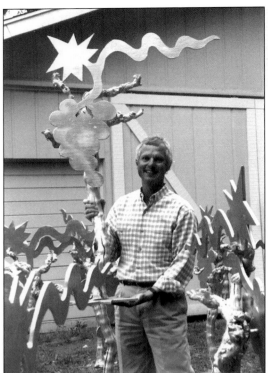

Each year the Napa Valley Museum hosts a pre-Wine Auction exhibit featuring works by local artists. Cary Gott, who was president of Sterling Vineyards when this picture was taken, displays some "fancified" vines. (Photo by Jana Russon; courtesy of the Napa Valley Vintner's Association.)

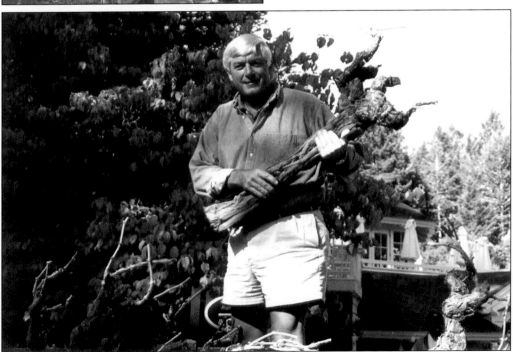

Grape grower Michael Beatty helps arrange an exhibit of vines. (Photo by Jana Russon; courtesy of the Napa Valley Vintner's Association.)

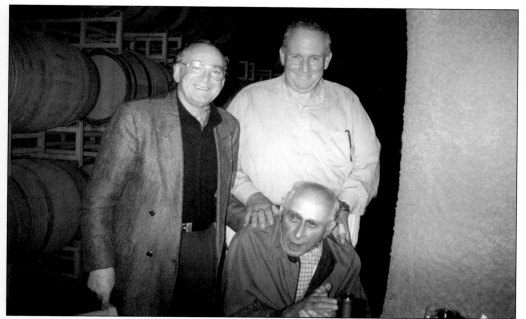

Jan Schrem (left) entertains visitors Leslie Rudd (Rudd Winery) and the seated Al Brounstein, (Diamond Creek Winery) at Schrem's Clos Pegase Winery. Schrem is one of several vintners who pair wine with fine art.

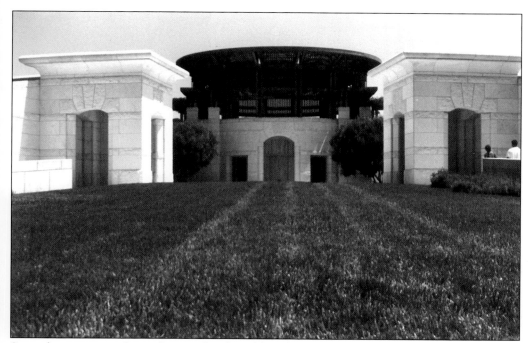

Several wineries are themselves works of art, like Clos Pegase and, shown here, Opus One.

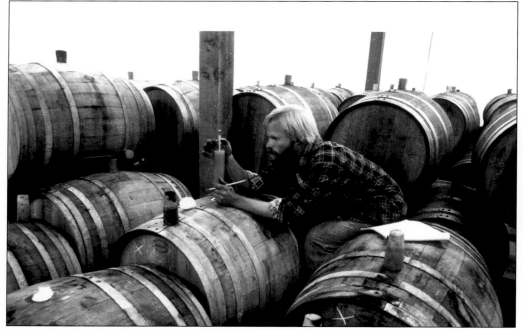

Banquets and celebrations are part of the Napa Valley lifestyle, but so is hard work. Here John Thomas tests the wine in barrels at Conn Creek Winery. (Photo by Susann Spann; courtesy of the Napa Valley Vintner's Association.)

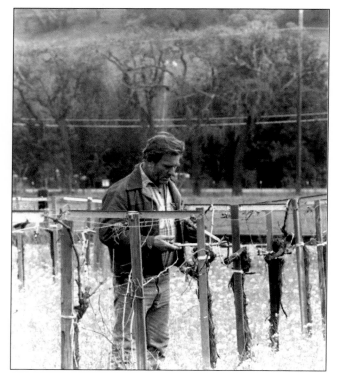

Grower Joseph Taddei stands knee-deep in mustard weed, pruning his vines. The Valley floor wears a brilliant yellow and green carpet in February and March. (Photo by Susann Spann; courtesy of the Napa Valley Vintner's Association.)

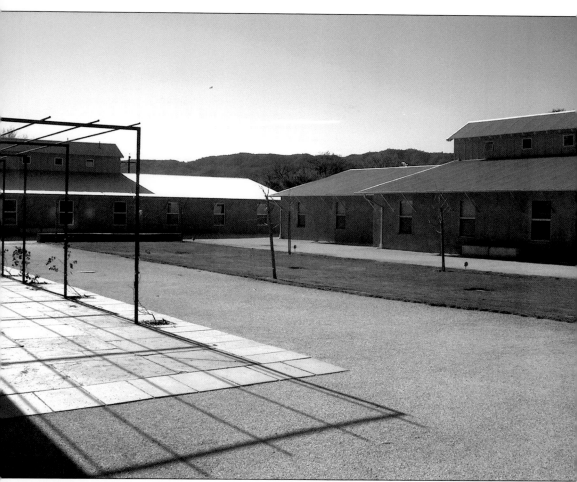

Farm workers represent an important and vital part of Napa's demographics. Without them, the wine industry could not function, and neither would the schools. Hispanic children make up 59.5 percent of all the children in Calistoga, and in St. Helena Hispanics account for about a third of the enrollment. Many farm workers are migrants. Joseph Phelps Winery recently donated land to build this housing for this seasonal population.

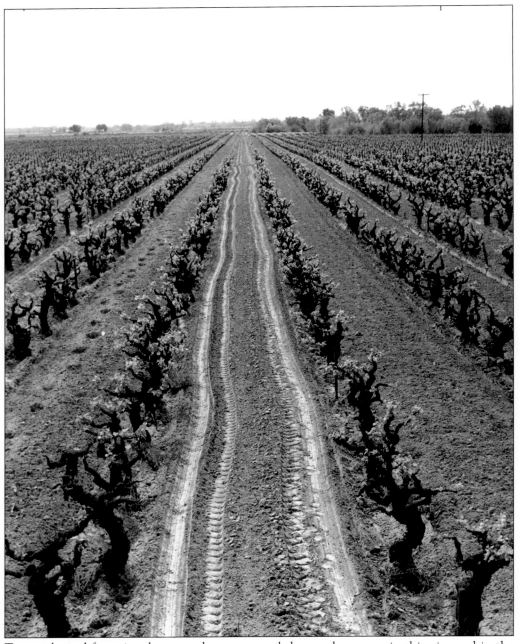

Tire marks and footprints between the rows reveal that work goes on in this vineyard in the early spring, as the vines push out their new buds. (Photo by Thomas Weber; courtesy of the Napa Valley Vintner's Association.)

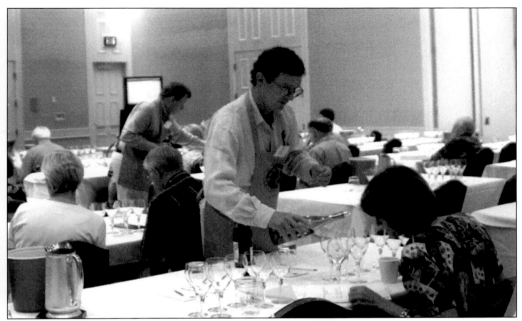

The Wine Library Association sponsors a magnificent wine tasting at the Silverado Country Club each year, where thousands of wine lovers come to sample hundreds of local wines. The day before the event, experts in the field offer seminars of interest to aficionados. Tasting is part of the experience. (Photo by Jim Cross, courtesy of the Wine Library Association.)

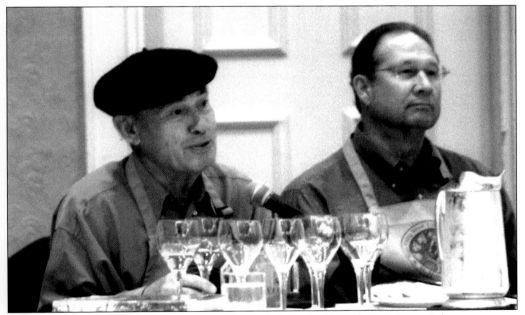

Vintner Mike Grgich (left) and vineyardist Bob Long hold forth at a Wine Library seminar. Before he founded Grgich Hills cellar, Mike worked at Chateau Montelena and made the Chardonnay that won the Paris tasting in 1976. (Photo by Jim Cross; courtesy of the Wine Library Association.)

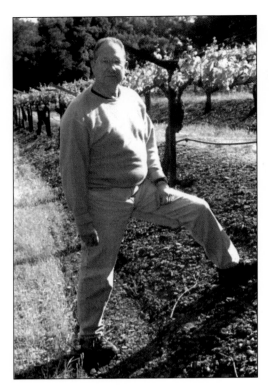

The cool evening breezes wafting across Lake Hennessey toward Pritchard Hill make conditions right for growing Chardonnay at Long Vineyards. Bob Long is CEO and founder. (Photo by Priscilla Upton; courtesy of the Wine Library Association.)

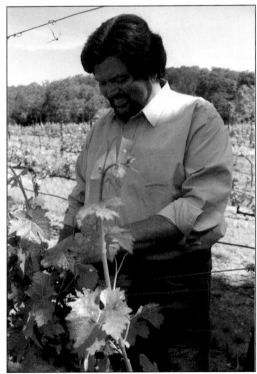

Ed Sbragia is the award-winning Winemaster at Beringer Blass Wine Estates. (Photo by Priscilla Upton; courtesy of the Wine Library Association.)

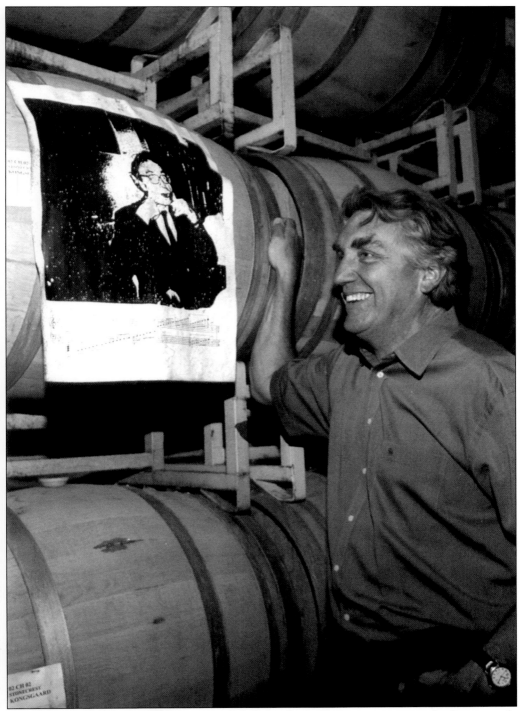

John Kongsgaard's roots go deep in Napa history, as his ancestors were among the first to settle here. John is a grower who also makes wine, both for himself and others. (Photo by Priscilla Upton; courtesy of the Wine Library Association.)

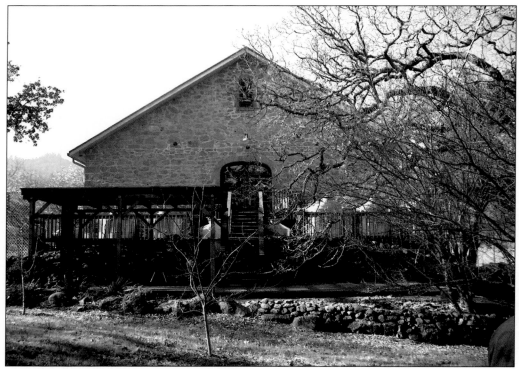

There are now more than 300 wineries in the Napa Valley, many of them small, family-owned ventures. Some, like Ehler's Lane, shown here, have changed hands several times.

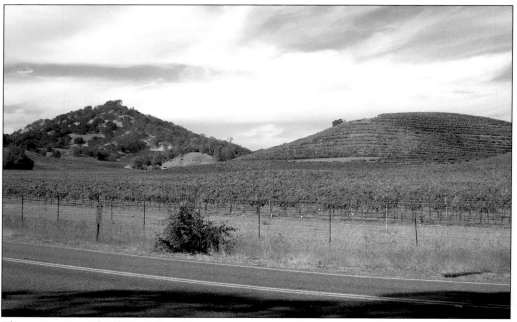

There are vineyards all over Napa County, even in areas once considered too remote. Cattle once grazed on these hillsides in Rancho Catacula, pioneer Joe Chiles's 1846 Mexican land grant.

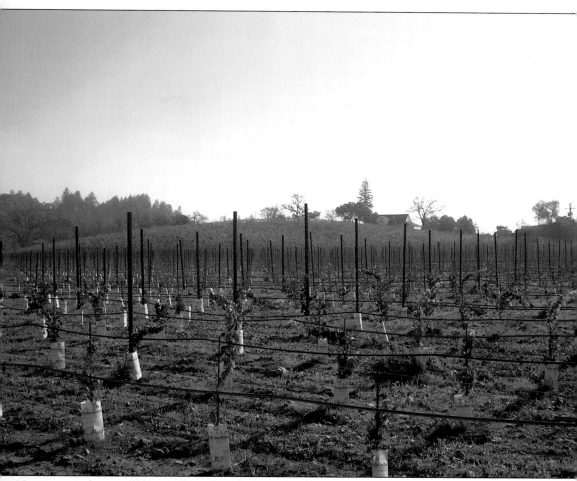

New vineyards are still being planted in the Napa Valley.

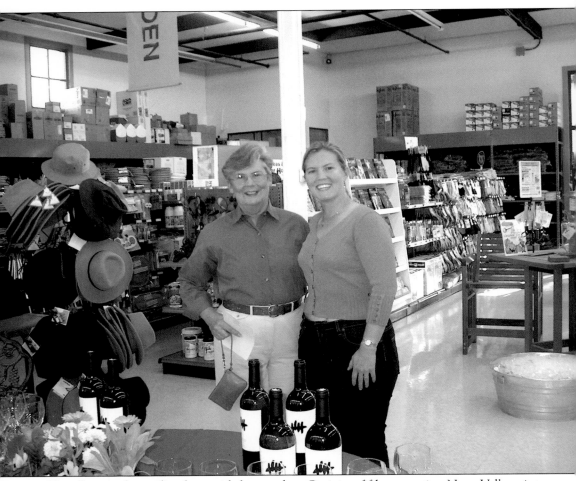

Krisi Raymond, standing here with her mother, Geri, is a fifth generation Napa Valley vintner. Her father is winemaker Walt Raymond (Raymond Winery). Her grandparents, Roy Raymond and Martha Jane Beringer Raymond, great-grandfather, Otto Beringer, and great-great grandfather, Jacob Beringer, have all been leaders in the wine industry. The occasion for this memento is the remodeling of Central Valley Builders Supply, operating in St. Helena for three generations.